ECONOMIC AND SOCIAL COMMISSION FOR ASIA AND THE PACIFIC

STATISTICAL PROFILES   No. 13

WOMEN IN SRI LANKA

A COUNTRY PROFILE

UNITED NATIONS
New York, 1997

ST/ESCAP/1766

UNITED NATIONS PUBLICATION

Sales No. E.97.II.F.25

ISBN 92-1-119761-9

The profile has been prepared under project BK-X20-3-214, on improving statistics on women in the ESCAP region.

FOREWORD

The call for the development of statistics and indicators on the situation of women has, for some time, been voiced in various global and regional forums. It was first recommended by the World Plan of Action for the Implementation of the Objectives of the International Women's Year, adopted in 1975. The recommendations of the World Plan of Action were reaffirmed and elaborated in the Programme of Action for the Second Half of the United Nations Decade for Women: Equality, Development and Peace. On various occasions, the Commission, stressing the importance of social and human development, has recognized the need for improved statistics and indicators on women. It has noted that better indicators are required to monitor the situation of women and to assess the effectiveness of strategies and programmes designed to address priority gender issues.

The secretariat initiated the project on improving statistics on women in the ESCAP region in 1994. The project aims to support governments in their efforts to promote the full integration of women in development and improve their status in line with the Nairobi Forward-looking Strategies for the Advancement of Women adopted in 1985. The project has been implemented by the Economic and Social Commission for Asia and the Pacific (ESCAP) through its subprogramme on statistics, with funding assistance from the Government of the Netherlands.

As a major component of its activities, the project commissioned experts from 19 countries in the region to prepare country profiles on the situation of women and men in the family, at work, and in public life, by analysing available statistical data and information. The profiles are intended to highlight the areas where action is needed, and to raise the consciousness of readers about issues concerning women and men. The 19 countries are Bangladesh, China, India, Indonesia, the Islamic Republic of Iran, Japan, Nepal, Pakistan, the Philippines, the Republic of Korea, Sri Lanka and Thailand in Asia; and Cook Islands, Fiji, Papua New Guinea, Samoa, Solomon Islands, Tonga and Vanuatu in the Pacific.

The secretariat hosted two meetings each in Asia and in the Pacific as part of the project activities. In the first meeting, the experts discussed and agreed on the structure, format and contents of the country profiles, based on guidelines prepared by the secretariat through Ms C.N. Ericta, consultant. The second meeting was a workshop to review the draft profiles. Participants in the workshop included the country experts and invited representatives from national statistical offices of Brunei Darussalam, Hong Kong, the Lao People's Democratic Republic, Mongolia and Viet Nam in Asia; of Marshall Islands, Tuvalu and Vanuatu in the Pacific; and representatives of United Nations organizations, specialized agencies and international organizations.

The original draft of the present profile, *Women in Sri Lanka,* was prepared by Mr Don Piyasena Wijegoonasekera, Consultant, Ministry of Women's Affairs. It was technically edited and modified by the ESCAP secretariat with the assistance of Mr S. Selvaratnam, consultant. The profiles express the views of the authors and not necessarily those of the secretariat.

I wish to express my sincere appreciation to the Government of the Netherlands for its generous financial support, which enabled the secretariat to implement the project.

Adrianus Mooy
Executive Secretary

CONTENTS

Page

Foreword iii

List of tables vi

List of figures xi

List of annex tables xii

PART I. DESCRIPTIVE ANALYSIS 1

    Introduction 3

    A. Highlights 5

    B. The setting 8

    C. Women's profile 16

    D. Women in family life 47

    E. Women in economic life 60

    F. Women in public life 77

PART II. ANNEX TABLES 87

References 95

LIST OF TABLES

Page

1. Annual rainfall, maximum and minimum temperatures at selected stations 9

2. Land utilization within agricultural holdings: Census of Agriculture, 1982 9

3. Percentage sectoral composition of gross domestic product in real terms
(1982 prices): 1985-1994 13

4. Growth of schooling facilities in Sri Lanka: 1945-1994 14

5. Number of government medical institutions and beds: 1991 15

6. Percentage of population covered by water supply and sanitation facilities,
by province and area 16

7. Enumerated population classified by sex, percentage female and sex ratio:
census years, 1871-1981 17

8. Registered live births by sex, percentage of female births and sex ratio at birth:
1901-1993 17

9. Age-specific death rates by gender: 1979 and 1989 18

10. Estimated and projected population by sex and sex ratio: 1985-2050 18

11. Sex ratios by broad age groups: census years of 1953 to 1981 19

12. Sex ratios by urban and rural residence: census years of 1953 to 1981 19

13. Distribution of the population by broad age group and sex: censuses of 1953
to 1981 and Demographic and Health Survey, 1993 20

14. Percentage distribution of men and women aged 15 years and over by marital
status: censuses of 1946 to 1981 21

15. Enrolment at primary and secondary levels (grades 1-13) by sex: 1911-1989 23

16. School enrolment by province and sex: 1985 and 1993 23

17. Percentage distribution of enrolment in various grades by sex: selected years,
1970-1993 23

18. Drop-out rates in government schools by educational level and sex: selected years,
1985-1992 24

19. Age-specific enrolment rates in schools by sex: population censuses of 1963 to 1981
and school census of 1991 25

20. Age-specific school enrolment rates by urban and rural areas and sex: 1981
population census 25

21. Enrolment in grades 12 and 13 by field of study and sex: 1992 26

22. Enrolment in technical colleges by course of study and sex: 1984 28

23. Student enrolment in universities by sex: 1942/43 to 1991/92 29

Page

24. Percentage distribution of university entrants by sex and parents' occupation: 1950 and 1977 29

25. Percentage share of women students in total undergraduate enrolment in universities by faculty: selected years, 1966/67 to 1991/92 30

26. Output of graduates from universities by field of study and sex: 1985 and 1990 31

27. Enrolment of postgraduate students in universities by course of study and sex: 1988/89 and 1991/92 31

28. Student enrolment in postgraduate and undergraduate institutions, by sex: 1985 and 1994 32

29. Enrolment in affliated university colleges by study course and sex: 1994 32

30. Student enrolment at the Open University by course of study and sex: 1988/89 and 1990/91 33

31. Teachers by qualifications and sex: 1985 and 1993 34

32. Academic staff of the universities by level and sex: 1991 34

33. Percentage distribution of persons aged 10 years and over by level of education completed and sex: censuses of 1963 to 1981 and sample surveys of 1985/86 and 1990/91 35

34. Percentage distribution of persons aged 10 years and over by educational level, sector and sex: 1985/86 36

35. Percentage of literate persons aged 10 years and over by sex: 1901-1991 36

36. Literacy rates by sector and sex: 1971-1990/91 37

37. Age-specific literacy rates by sex: 1985/86 and 1990/91 37

38. Incidence of moderate and severe malnutrition in children: 1987 and 1993 39

39. Percentage distribution of newborn babies by birthweight and by province and residence: 1988/89 39

40. Mean birthweight and incidence of low birthweight by background characteristics: 1993 40

41. Crude death rate by sex: selected years, 1941-1989 41

42. Death rates by age group and sex: 1973, 1980 and 1989 41

43. Cause-specific mortality rates for selected diseases by sex: 1984 and 1989 42

44. Infant mortality rate by sex: selected years, 1900-1988 42

45. Infant mortality rate by ethnic group and sex: 1976, 1982 and 1988 43

46. Mortality rate for children aged 1-4 years by residence and sex: 1980-1988 44

47. Maternal mortality by age group: selected years, 1971-1988 44

48. Percentage distribution of births in the five years preceding the 1993 Demographic and Health Survey, by place of delivery and residence 45

LIST OF TABLES *(continued)*

Page

49. Percentage distribution of births in the five years prior to the 1993 Demographic and Health Survey, by type of assistance mother received during delivery and residence 45

50. Maternal mortality by province: selected years, 1976-1988 46

51. Percentage distribution of maternal deaths by major cause: 1980, 1985 and 1988 46

52. Estimates of life expectancy at birth by sex 47

53. Percentage of female-headed households by district: 1981 and 1994 48

54. Percentage distribution of household heads by marital status and gender: 1981 and 1994 48

55. Percentage distribution of male and female household heads by age group and residence: 1993 49

56. Percentage distribution of male and female household heads by household size and residence: 1993 49

57. Percentage of never-married men and women at selected age groups: censuses of 1946 to 1981 50

58. Percentage of never-married women at ages 15-49: 1987 and 1993 51

59. Percentage of never-married youth aged 15-19 years and average age at first marriage by sex for selected countries 52

60. Singulate mean age at marriage by sex: 1901-1993 52

61. Males per 100 females in selected age groups: censuses of 1911 to 1981 and Demographic and Health Survey, 1987 53

62. Percentage distribution of women by type of marriage, level of educational attainment and generation: 1985 54

63. Age-specific fertility rates and total fertility rate: 1963 to 1988-1993 55

64. Mean number of children ever born for women aged 45-49 years: 1975-1993 55

65. Percentage of ever-married and currently married women aged 15-49 knowing any method, any modern method and any traditional method of contraception: Demographic and Health Surveys of 1987 and 1993 56

66. Percentage of currently married women aged 15-49 years knowing any method, any modern method and any traditional method of contraception, by current age of women: 1993 56

67. Percentage of ever-married women who have ever used a contraceptive method, by major method: 1975-1993 57

68. Trends in current contraceptive use by method among currently married women aged 15-49 years: 1975-1993 57

69. Age-specific proportions of widowed and divorced/separated persons by sex: 1981 census 58

Page

70. Marriages by type and civil condition: 1983, 1985 and 1988 59

71. Numerical and percentage distribution of reported cases of domestic violence
against women by broad category of offence: 1990 and 1991 60

72. Overall labour-force participation rates of persons aged 10 years and over by sex:
censuses of 1963 to 1981 and Labour Force Surveys of 1885/86, 1992, 1995 and 1996 62

73. Labour-force participation rates by age group and sex: 1971-1995 62

74. Labour-force participation rate by sex and residence: 1963-1995 63

75. Percentage distribution of the labour force by activity status and gender:
1963-1996 64

76. Employment rates of the labour force by age group and sex: 1981, 1985/86
and 1992 65

77. Percentage distribution of employed persons aged 10 years and over by major
industrial sector and sex: 1981 and 1995 66

78. Percentage distribution of employed persons aged 10 years and over by employment
status and sex: 1981, 1985/86, 1991 and 1995 66

79. Percentage distribution of currently employed persons by hours per week actually
worked at the main job and by gender: 1995 67

80. Percentage distribution of unemployed persons by age group and sex: 1971-1992 68

81. Age-specific unemployment rates by sex: Labour Force Surveys of 1985/86,
1990 and 1995 68

82. Percentage distribution of the unemployed by level of educational attainment
and sex: 1985/86, 1994 and 1995 69

83. Unemployment rates by educational level and sex: 1985/86 and 1994 70

84. Percentage distribution of unemployed persons by duration of unemployment
and sex for various occupations desired: 1995 70

85. Numerical and percentage distribution of persons aged 10 years and over currently
not in the labour force by age group and sex: first quarter, 1995 71

86. Percentage distribution of persons aged 10 years and over currently not in the
labour force, by reason and by age group and sex: first quarter, 1995 72

87. Sri Lankan nationals emigrating as migrant workers, by sex: 1988-1995 73

88. Estimated stock of Sri Lankan overseas contract workers by country of
employment and gender: 1996 74

89. Sri Lankan nationals emigrating as temporary labour migrants, by occupational
category and sex: 1988-1995 75

90. Distribution of Sri Lankan women employed as housemaids in foreign countries
by country of employment: 1988-1995 75

Page

91. Sri Lankan nationals emigrating as temporary migrant workers by age group, marital status and source of employment: 1994 76

92. Migrant workers by reason for seeking employment abroad and by sex: 1986 76

93. Use of remittances by a sample of women worker migrants to the Middle East in two urban localities of Sri Lanka 76

94. Numerical and percentage distribution of complaints from Sri Lankan women working abroad, by nature of complaint and sector of employment: 1985-1990 77

95. Numerical and percentage distribution of candidates contesting elections to Parliament, provincial councils and local authorities, by sex: 1977-1989 78

96. Parliament membership by sex: 1965-1994 79

97. Women in local government councils: 1991 and 1994 80

98. Participation of women at the ministerial level: 1980-1994 81

99. Distribution of Secretary-level positions by level and sex: 1980, 1985 and 1993 81

100. Distribution of officers in the Sri Lanka Administrative Service by level and sex: 1979 and 1993 82

101. Distribution of members of the Sri Lanka Scientific Service by level and sex: 1984 and 1995 82

102. Distribution of officers in the Sri Lanka Planning Service by level and sex: 1979, 1988 and 1995 83

103. Representation of women in the foreign missions of Sri Lanka: 1980-1993 83

104. Numerical and percentage distribution of government employees by sector and sex: 1980, 1985 and 1990 84

105. Numerical and percentage distribution of government employees by occupational group and sex: 1990 85

106. Men and women at the Bar: 1985 and 1992 85

107. Judges in the lower courts, by sex: 1985, 1990 and 1993 86

108. Distribution of police personnel, by sex: 1980, 1985, 1990 and 1993 86

LIST OF FIGURES

Page

1. Structure of the Sri Lankan Government 10

2. Population growth by sex: 1871-1981 11

3. Median age of the population by sex: 1946-1993 20

4. School drop-out rates at primary and secondary levels of education by sex:
   selected years, 1985-1992 24

5. Performance at the General Certificate of Education Ordinary Level and
   General Certificate of Education Advanced Level Examinations, by sex: 1994 27

6. Literacy rates of population aged 10 years and over by sex: 1901-1981 36

7. Infant mortality rate by ethnic group and sex: 1988 43

8. Difficulties perceived by female heads of households 49

9. Labour-force participation rate by age and sex: 1992 63

LIST OF ANNEX TABLES

Page

A. HIGHLIGHTS

(no annex tables)

B. THE SETTING

B.1 Land area, estimated mid-year population and population density by province and district: 1995 89

C. WOMEN'S PROFILE

C.1 Numerical distribution of the enumerated population by five-year age group and sex: census years of 1953 to 1981 90

C.2 Percentage distribution of the enumerated population by five-year age group and sex: census years of 1953 to 1981 90

C.3 Numerical distribution of persons aged 15 years and over by marital status and sex: census years of 1946 to 1981 90

C.4 Drop-out rates up to year 9 in government schools by province, district and sex: 1991/92 91

C.5 Trainees in vocational training courses under the National Apprenticeship and Industrial Training Authority, by type of course and sex: 1992 92

C.6 Distribution of university undergraduate students by faculty and sex: selected years, 1966/67 to 1991/92 92

C.7 Infant mortality rates by district and sex: 1970, 1980 and 1988 93

D. WOMEN IN FAMILY LIFE

D.1 Percentage of currently married women by current use of contraception and background characteristics: 1993 94

E. WOMEN IN ECONOMIC LIFE

E.1 Total population and economically active population aged 10 years and over by activity status and sex: 1963-1996 94

F. WOMEN IN PUBLIC LIFE

(no annex tables)

PART I
DESCRIPTIVE ANALYSIS

INTRODUCTION

In Sri Lanka, the status of women is somewhat paradoxical. Judged in terms of relevant indicators, the physical well-being of Sri Lankan women is far superior to that of women in most other developing countries. For instance, their expectation of life at birth, which is higher than that of their male counterparts, and literacy rates, approximate those of the developed countries. Within the family, Sri Lankan women are less vulnerable to discrimination and oppression than other women in the South Asian region. Son preference is not so evident and extreme cases of male dominance, such as dowry deaths and widow immolation, are absent. Traditionally, Sri Lankan women have also not been subjected to repugnant socio-cultural practices such as purdah (female seclusion), circumcision, footbinding, child marriage, polygamy etc. which have been and continue to be prevalent to varying degrees in several countries of the region. For these reasons, it has often been believed and stated publicly that Sri Lankan females enjoy a status equal to that of their male counterparts in various spheres of life. But in most respects their status is similar to that of women in other Asian countries: one of general subordination in a male-dominated society.

Sri Lanka has ratified several relevant international covenants, including the United Nations Convention on the Elimination of All Forms of Discrimination Against Women, without any reservation. The 1978 Constitution seeks to guarantee freedom from discrimination on grounds of sex and also recognizes that the State may take affirmative action for the advancement of women. Yet, only new legislation can be challenged on the grounds of gender discrimination; the Constitution does not provide for power of judicial review of past legislation which has discriminated against women. For example, the 1936 Land Development Ordinance and subsequent amendments to it continue to erode the traditional rights of women to land ownership in settlement areas.

Customary, personal or family laws continue to impinge strongly on the lives of women in respect of their inheritance rights as well as marriage, divorce and custody of children. By and large, these laws reflect the traditional or religious practices of different ethnic groups, and range from the relatively more liberal Sinhalese or "Kandyan" law to the Thesavalamai laws governing the Jaffna Tamils, and to the more stringent Muslim laws under which, for example, men can take unilateral action in divorce, and a female inherits half the share of a male. An overall commitment to the protection of the cultural and religious rights of various groups appears to have hampered the adoption of uniform norms and standards for the country as a whole.

Although the various labour laws of the country are in consonance with internationally agreed practices, and maternity leave has been extended from six weeks to three months for the first two pregnancies, these laws are enforced only in the larger establishments in the public and private sectors. Consequently, women, who constitute the majority of workers in the smaller establishments and in the unorganized and informal sectors, are not covered by the labour legislation and are therefore vulnerable to exploitation and harassment by employers and entrepreneurs. Similarly, the outdated laws relating to rape and trafficking in women are considered to be ineffective in coping with contemporary problems.

In recognition of the need to address the various problems and issues faced by women in a systematic manner, several voluntary organizations concerned with the improvement of the status of women made representations to the government in the late 1970s urging the establishment of a central body to advise it in regard to the formulation of policies and programmes for the increased participation of women in development, as well as to coordinate and monitor programmes aimed at enhancing the status of women. In response to this request, a Women's Bureau was established in October 1978 as a specialized agency functioning within the then Ministry of Plan Implementation, which was directly under the Executive President. The main functions of the Women's Bureau were to work for the improvement of the quality of life of women, act as a link between organizations concerned with women's issues and the government, advise the government on the formulation of official policy, and monitor the implementation of such policy.

In 1983, women's affairs were made a matter of ministerial concern and assigned to a woman Minister who headed the Ministry of Women's Affairs and Teaching Hospitals. With the change of President after the 1989 elections and the relocation of portfolios, the Women's Bureau became a unit of the State Ministry of Women's Affairs, which functioned under the Cabinet Ministry of Health and Women's Affairs.

The National Strategy for Women developed and adopted in 1988 recommended that the Women's Bureau should operate at the national level in areas such as advocacy, information collection, research, coordination and monitoring. With the setting up of the provincial councils in 1989, ministries on women's affairs were also established at all provincial levels to direct, coordinate and monitor women in development activities.

In 1991-1992, the Ministry of Women's Affairs, in collaboration with concerned non-governmental organizations, formulated the Women's Charter of Sri Lanka to ensure "the full development and advancement of women, for the purpose of guaranteeing them the exercise and enjoyment of human rights and fundamental freedoms on a basis of equality with men". The Charter was approved by the Cabinet as a state policy in March 1983 but has yet to receive legal validity by Parliament. Under the terms of article 17 of the Charter, the President appointed a National Committee on Women comprising 14 members, both males and females, representing a very wide spectrum of expertise and activities. The Committee has been mandated, among other things, to monitor the progress in regard to implementation of

the Women's Charter, to receive complaints of gender discrimination and other issues and problems of women, and to help formulate strategies to resolve them. It is expected that the National Committee will be upgraded to a National Commission by an Act of Parliament in the near future.

The new government that came into power in 1994 had made women's concerns the responsibility of the Women's Affairs Division of the Ministry of Transport, Environment and Women's Affairs, headed by a woman Minister. Recently, the Division formulated a National Plan of Action for Women in Sri Lanka. This Plan focuses on problems and issues which are of critical and specific concern to women in the country and sets out strategies and activities for resolving them.

The establishment of the Ministry of Women's Affairs, the acceptance of the Women's Charter as state policy, the setting up of the National Committee on Women to monitor the implementation of the Charter, and to advise the government on the formulation of appropriate policies on women's issues, as well as the preparation and publication of the National Plan of Action for Women in Sri Lanka, clearly reflect the commitment towards and the priorities accorded to women's concerns and issues by successive Sri Lankan governments since 1977. However, there is a long way to go in bridging the gap between the legitimate grievances and aspirations of women and the policies and measures so far implemented towards mitigating these grievances.

The systematic monitoring of existing policies and programmes related to the enhancement of women's status in the country, as well as the formulation and implementation of additional measures required to bring about equality between men and women in various social and economic fields, call for the collection and analysis of relevant data and information on a continuing basis. Fortunately, a large amount of statistical data pertaining to women's concerns is being routinely collected and processed in Sri Lanka, although some of the data need to be disaggregated by gender. There is also a need to initiate the collection and analysis of additional data in certain areas of women's concerns in the country.

The present profile on women in Sri Lanka attempts to bring together available data and information collected by various agencies, or provided through research studies, to give as comprehensive a picture as possible of the progress so far made in regard to enhancing the participation of women in various social, economic and cultural development programmes and the extent to which these programmes have succeeded in ensuring equality between men and women in the social, economic and political spheres. It is hoped that this profile will, with appropriate modifications, serve as a framework for the continuing analysis and assessment of the situation in regard to the status of women in Sri Lanka.

A. HIGHLIGHTS

The setting

1.   The island Republic of Sri Lanka has a total land area of 65,614 square kilometres and is characterized by three distinct physical features: a mountain region in the central and south-western part; an upland belt surrounding the mountain country; and a flat constant belt. Nearly 30 per cent of the total area constitutes developed agricultural land, almost half of which is under tea, rubber and coconut.

2.   The country has a presidential system of government akin to the French model, with the elected President being head of state, head of government, head of cabinet and commander-in-chief of the armed forces. For convenience of administration, the country is divided into 8 provinces and 25 districts.

3.   The estimated population of 17.9 million in 1995 is composed of several ethnic and religious groups. Nearly two thirds of the people live in the south-western part of the country, which constitutes about 26 per cent of the country's land area. An estimated 23 per cent reside in areas nationally defined as urban.

4.   Sri Lanka is a developing economy with a per capita gross national product (GNP) estimated at US$ 570 in 1993. The agricultural sector has been the mainstay of the national economy for a long time and is still important, despite its declining share of gross domestic product (GDP). In recent years, the manufacturing sector has assumed increasing importance, with its share of GDP rising from 14.8 per cent in 1985 to 19.7 per cent in 1994. Recent surveys indicate that about 30 per cent of the country's households live in absolute poverty.

5.   Sri Lanka's distinctive pattern of development, with its emphasis on human resources development, has resulted in the establishment of an expanding island-wide network of educational and health institutions and services within easy access of people living in urban as well as rural areas.

Women's profile

1.   For a long time in the past, males had consistently outnumbered females in the total population. However, in recent decades, this numerical gap between the sexes has been gradually narrowing owing to greater reduction in female than male mortality, resulting in a slight excess of females over males, according to 1995 estimates.

2.   As a result of changes in fertility and mortality patterns, there have been significant shifts in the age structure of the population, with a decline in the relative share of young children and youth and a rise in the proportion of persons in working ages. There has also been a steady rise in the proportion of women in the reproductive ages 15-49 years; today, over 50 per cent of the country's females are concentrated in this age cohort.

3.   The median age of the population has also been rising steadily over the years; in 1993, the median age for females was one year more than for males.

4.   A higher percentage among women compared with men aged 15 years and over were

reported to be married. The incidence of marital disruption owing to widowhood or divorce/separation is also higher among women than men.

5. Although boys outnumber girls in total primary school enrolments, more girls than boys are enrolled at the higher levels. The enrolment ratio of 63.4 per cent for girls aged 5-24 years was slightly higher than the corresponding rate for boys in 1963.

6. The drop-out rates at primary and secondary levels are lower for girls than for boys. Generally, girls have been performing better than boys at the General Certificate of Education examinations.

7. Females not only continue to be underrepresented in several study courses at the vocational and technical institutions but are also largely concentrated in those courses related to occupations in the service sector.

8. The proportionate share of females in total enrolments at the universities has increased steadily, from 10 per cent in 1942/43 to 44.4 per cent in 1991/92. This increase has been accompanied by a radical change in the socio-economic background of students entering the university; today the majority of these entrants are from low-income families.

9. Despite the increasing participation of females in higher education, gender stereotyping in regard to selection of subject courses persists, with a predominance of girls in arts-based courses and of boys in science-based courses.

10. The proportion of females aged 10 years and over with no schooling has declined to almost a third, from 33.8 per cent in 1963 to 11.3 per cent in 1991, and the female literacy rate of 83.8 per cent in 1990/91 is among the highest in the world.

11. Undernutrition appears to be a problem affecting children and expectant mothers. A 1988/89 Nutritional Survey indicated that about a fifth of the newborn babies were underweight, this proportion being considerably higher in rural than in urban areas.

12. While in the past the mortality rates for females were higher than those for males in all age groups, since the 1960s female rates have been lower than male rates.

13. There have been sharp reductions in infant and child mortality rates over the years owing to the expansion of the immunization programmes. Maternal mortality rates have also fallen drastically over the years and the current rates are comparable with those prevailing in more advanced countries. About 94 per cent of all birth deliveries take place under the supervision of professionally trained medical personnel.

14. The female life expectancy at birth of 74.2 years in 1991 is nearly five years longer than male life expectancy.

Women in family life

1. The proportion of female household heads had increased from 17.4 per cent in 1981 to 18.6 per cent in 1994. In 1994, about 58 per cent of the female household heads were either widowed or divorced/separated, and a little over half of them were aged 60 years and over.

2. There have been significant changes over the years in the marriage patterns in the country, with an increasing proportion of girls in the marriageable ages remaining unmarried. In 1993, about 93 per cent of girls at ages 15-19 were reported to be unmarried. This proportion approximates the corresponding level reported for Ireland in 1988.

3. The singulate mean age at marriage for females increased from 18.3 years in 1901 to 25.5 years in 1993. Increasing female participation in education and employment, as well as non-availability of male partners at appropriate marriage ages, are considered to have contributed to the increasing proportion of single women at younger age groups and to the increasing age at first marriage.

4. Another reported change in marriage practices is the transition from arranged to love marriages; the incidence of romantic marriages

increased from about 25 per cent of the unions in the 1940s to about 52 per cent in the late 1980s.

5. Remarkable changes are taking place in the reproductive behaviour of Sri Lankan women, as reflected in the reduction in the total fertility rate (TFR) from 5.0 children per woman in 1963 to 2.3 in 1988-1993. This decline has largely been brought about by the increasing practice of contraception among currently married women.

6. Successive surveys reveal a rise in knowledge about contraception among women in reproductive ages which is now almost universal. These surveys also show that the proportion of currently married women aged 15-49 years currently using a contraceptive method had almost doubled, from 34.4 per cent in 1975 to 66.1 per cent in 1993.

7. The overall incidence of marital disruption owing to widowhood or divorce/separation is relatively low in Sri Lanka. Recent marriage data also indicate an increasing number of re-marriages of widows and divorced women in the country.

8. Domestic violence against women and female children is reported to be on the rise. Another area of concern is the increasing incidence of incest.

Women in economic life

1. Although Sri Lankan women constitute about half the national population of working ages, they represent only about a third of the country's workforce or persons who are deemed to be economically active. In 1996, the labour-force participation rate for females was 33.5 per cent, compared with 65.3 per cent for males.

2. There has, however, been a very significant increase in female labour-force participation since 1963 in absolute as well as relative terms. However, a substantial portion of this increase has been in the categories of casual employees and unpaid family workers.

3. Female labour-force participation is significantly higher in rural compared with urban areas because the rural areas also include the estate sector, in which women constitute half the plantation labour force, and because of the tendency to report women in farm households as unpaid family workers.

4. Although an increasing number of women have found employment in recent times, they tend to be concentrated in low-paid, low-skill and low-status jobs in peasant and plantation agriculture, in small-scale industries and in petty trade and domestic services. A higher proportion among women than men also work as unpaid family workers.

5. The unemployment rate among women is also considerably higher than that among men. The unemployed females also have to wait, on an average, for a longer period than their male counterparts before finding a job.

6. The disadvantageous situation in which women are placed in regard to employment vis-à-vis men in Sri Lanka is largely due to the perception among planners, policy makers and administrators that women are dependent housewives, or at best, secondary earners within the family.

7. A recent phenomenon is the increasing number of Sri Lankan women migrating to the Middle East and developed countries to work as housemaids. Their remittances have enabled them not only to enhance the well-being of their immediate family members but also to augment the country's foreign exchange earnings.

Women in public life

1. Although as registered as well as actual voters women are almost equal in number to men, their participation in the political processes as candidates contesting elections is very low. Consequently, women are very much under-represented in the various legislative organs at the national, provincial and local levels.

2. A recent phenomenon, however, has been the active participation of women in militarized

political movements such as the Janatha Vimukthi Peramuna (JVP) and the Liberation Tigers of Tamil Eelam (LTTE).

3. The participation of women in decision-making at various levels is very low. Although a woman is currently head of the State and head of government, less than 10 per cent of Cabinet-level ministers and about 17 per cent of non-Cabinet-level ministers of the government are women. No woman has to date been appointed to function as Secretary of a Cabinet-level ministry.

4. Although an increasing number of women have been recruited to the Sri Lanka Administrative Service, the Sri Lanka Scientific Service and the Sri Lanka Planning Service, most of them are concentrated in the lower levels of these services. Women occupy only about 10-13 per cent of positions at the highest level in these services.

5. There is only one woman among the 34 Ambassadors/High Commissioners in the foreign service, and even among the lower-level diplomatic positions only about 16 per cent are occupied by women.

6. The relative share of women in government service increased from 22.3 per cent in 1980 to 29.7 per cent in 1990, and nearly 58 per cent of female government servants fall under the occupational category of professionals, which include teachers, nurses, midwives etc.

7. An increasing number of women are qualifying as attorneys and the number of women enrolled at the Bar more than doubled between 1985 and 1992. Women are also being appointed as judges, particularly to the Lower Courts, where they now constitute about 23 per cent of the total number of judges.

8. Since 1953, women have been enlisted into the police force, particularly at the lowest levels, but after 40 years women still constitute only about 3.5 per cent of the total. They also account for about one per cent of army, 2.7 per cent of air force and 2.0 per cent of navy personnel.

B. THE SETTING

1. Location and physical features

The island Republic of Sri Lanka, formerly known as Ceylon, is situated in the Indian ocean between northern latitudes 5°5' and 9°50' and eastern longitudes 79°42' and 81°52'. It is separated from the southern part of the Indian subcontinent by a narrow strip of shallow water, the Palk Strait, and the Gulf of Mannar. Besides India, Sri Lanka's nearest neighbours are Maldives to the west and the Indian territories of Nicobar and the Andaman Islands to the east and north-east respectively.

The pear-shaped island country extends through its greatest length 435 kilometres (270 miles) from Point Palmyrah in the north to Dondra Head in the south. Its greatest width is 225 kilometres (140 miles) from Colombo in the west to Sangamankande on the east coast. The total area of the country is 65,614 square kilometres, or 25,332 square miles, of which about 1,156 square kilometres, or 320 square miles, comprise large inland waters.

The relief of the island constitutes a mountainous area covering the south and central part and ranging in elevation from 900 to 2,100 metres (3,000 to 7,000 feet) where most of the tea and rubber plantations are located; a coastal belt which is narrow in the east, south and west, but fans out in the north reaching from the eastern to the western shores of the country; and an intermediate upland belt between the two areas surrounding the central hills with an elevation of about 300 to 900 metres (1,000 to 3,000 feet).

2. Climate and rainfall

Sri Lanka has temperatures appropriate to its near-equatorial position, modified by altitude. The mean monthly temperatures in most of the country range from 26°C to 28°C in the plains. The elevated areas are cooler, with a greater range; at Nuwara Eliya, which is 1,889 metres above sea level, temperatures range between 14°C in January and 16°C in May.

Rainfall is the most important element in the climate; climatic variations in different places are the result of the seasonal incidence of rainfall. Although the country is divided into two climatic zones, the dry zone, which is largely the north-eastern section covering about 64 per cent of the country, and the wet zone, comprising the south-western sections, no part of the country is completely dry. In the wet zone, annual rainfall varies from 1,900 to 2,500 milimetres, while in the dry zone it ranges from 900 to 1,900 milimetres.

3. Land-use patterns

According to the data from the 1982 Census of Agriculture, nearly 40 per cent of the land area within agricultural holdings is devoted to the cultivation of the three major export crops, tea, rubber and coconut, a further 27.7 per cent is devoted to paddy cultivation, and another 18.5 per cent used for other crops, both permanent and temporary. Forests and pasture lands occupy 4.7 per cent of the land area, while another 4.6 per cent which is cultivable remains uncultivated (table 2).

4. Government and administration

For over 300 years since 1505, the maritime provinces of the country came under successive foreign colonial powers: Portugese (1505-1640), Dutch (1640-1796), and British (1796-1948). Much of the interior of the island remained independent under the Kandyan kings. The Kandyan Kingdom was absorbed into the British

Colony of Ceylon in 1815-1818, when for the first time one foreign power controlled all of Sri Lanka. The country regained its independence in 1948 through a process of peaceful constitutional evolution.

Since independence, Sri Lanka has had three constitutional systems. The Soulbury Constitution, introduced by the outgoing British colonial power, was a replica of the British Westminster model with the British monarch as head of state, executive power in the hands of a prime minister governing in cabinet, and a bicameral legislature. The second Constitution, adopted in 1972, did not deviate much

Table 2. Land utilization within agricultural holdings: Census of Agriculture, 1982

Type of land use	Area	
	Hectares	Percentage
Tea, rubber and coconut	798 103	39.7
Other permanent crops	176 500	8.8
Paddy	556 982	27.7
Temporary crops other than paddy	195 048	9.7
Wood and forest land	54 129	2.7
Pasture land	20 097	1.0
Cultivable area uncultivated	91 648	4.6
Roads and buildings	75 416	3.7
Rocky and waste land area	40 805	2.1
Total	2 008 728	100.0

Source: Department of Census and Statistics, *Census of Agriculture, 1982.*

Table 1. Annual rainfall, maximum and minimum temperatures at selected stations

Station	Annual rainfall (mm)		Annual temperature (degrees C)			
	Average 1961-1990	1995	Average 1951-1980		1995	
			Maximum	Minimum	Maximum	Minimum
Colombo	2 425.8	2 398.9	30.4	24.0	31.2	24.7
Trincomalee	1 580.0	1 379.4	31.1	25.2	32.6	25.0
Hambantota	1 049.6	962.8	30.2	24.1	30.9	24.4
Ratnapura	3 749.1	4 115.9	31.9	22.7	31.7	22.8
Anuradhapura	1 284.5	849.4	31.9	23.1	32.9	23.9
Katugastota	1 840.1	1 835.3	28.7	20.2	28.9	20.6
Bandavawela	1 571.9	1 388.2	n.a.	n.a.	25.2	16.6
Nuwara Eliya	1 905.1	2 082.5	20.2	11.4	20.1	12.3

Source: Department of Census and Statistics, *Statistical Pocket Book of the Democratic Socialist Republic of Sri Lanka, 1996.*

n.a. = not available.

from the Westminster type except that the name of the country was changed from Ceylon to Sri Lanka, the country became a republic although remaining within the Commonwealth, and the bicameral legislature became unicameral. The executive power continued to be vested in the Prime Minister and the Cabinet, although a President was the constitutional head of state.

The third Constitution, adopted in 1978, altered some basic features of the system of government as well as the institutional division of power. This Constitution, which is somewhat similar to the French model, introduced a presidential system of government with the elected President as head of state, head of government, head of the cabinet of ministers, commander-in-chief of the armed forces, and leader of the ruling party. The powers of the Prime Minister and of the Cabinet, appointed by the President from among members of Parliament, were drastically reduced. A system of proportional representation was introduced to replace the previous "first-past-the-post" system of voting in elections.

In 1987, the Constitution was amended to provide for a system of devolution of political and administrative powers to the provinces within the framework of a unitary state. The scheme of devolution envisaged seeks to carve out an area of legislative, executive and financial competence at the provincial level. The scheme created eight provincial councils whose members are elected by the people. While the legislative powers are vested in these councils, executive powers are in the hands of the governors appointed by the President of Sri Lanka. A Board of Ministers, headed by a Chief Minister, assists and advises the governor in the exercise of his functions. The provincial councils, however, cannot override the legislative authority of the Parliament at the centre.

The separation of subjects and functions between the central government and provincial councils has been set out in three lists under the Ninth Schedule of the Constitution: the provincial council list, delineating the exclusive domain of devolved authority; the concurrent list, comprising subjects shared with the government; and the reserved list, setting out areas reserved for the government. Subjects and functions assigned to the provincial councils comprise mainly matters of regional concern and focus directly on the daily life of the people.

The districts, which now number 25, are the main administrative units. The district administration, with the Government Agent as the focal point, constitutes the outreach of the central government development programmes. Most of the ministries have district-level offices which constitute the middle and lower tiers of a centralized multilateral structure. The Government Agent, the Assistant Government Agent at the divisional level and the Grama Sevaka Niladhari (village-level officer) at the village level provide the backbone of the district administration (see also figure 1). The local government institutions, the town councils and village councils were reconstituted in the 1970s into Pradeshiya Mandala and Gramodaya Mandala.

Figure 1. Structure of the Sri Lankan Government

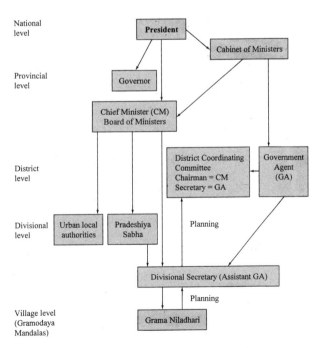

Source: Ministry of Public Administration, Provincial Councils and Home Affairs.

5. Population growth and distribution

The population of Sri Lanka has been enumerated at 12 censuses held between 1871 and 1981. According to these censuses, the population had increased more than fourfold from 2.4 million in 1871 to 14.8 million in 1981 (see figure 2). The 1990 round of population censuses has so far not been carried out owing to the continued civil war in the northern and eastern parts of the country. However, official estimates give a population of about 17 million in 1990 and 18.1 million in 1995. Recent estimates prepared by the United Nations also indicate a population of 17 million in 1990 and 17.9 million in 1995.

Figure 2. Population growth by sex: 1871-1981

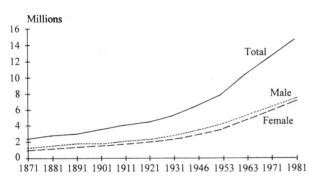

Source: ESCAP, *Socio-economic Profile of SAARC Countries: A Statistical Analysis,* Statistical Profiles No. 1 (Bangkok, 1996) (ST/ESCAP/1537).

Available data indicate that there was a sudden acceleration in the country's population growth between 1946 and 1963, when annual growth rates averaged more than 2.5 per cent, compared with 1.5 per cent in the period 1931-1946. This spurt in population has been attributed largely to the dramatic decline in mortality rates resulting from a vigorous and highly successful malaria eradication programme and from expansion and improvement in health services. There has also been a gradual decline in the rate of growth of the population since the 1950s; this decline has been more marked since the 1960s owing to a greater decline in fertility rates than in mortality rates. The annual growth rate over the period 1990-1995 is estimated at 1.27 per cent.

The overall density of 281 persons per square kilometre in 1995 masks the wide disparity in population distribution among the 25 administrative districts. The number of persons per square kilometre varies from 40 in Mullaitivu district in Northern Province to a high of 3,190 in Colombo district in Western Province. The density of Colombo district is nearly three times that of the next most populous district, Gampaha, also in Western Province (annex table B.1).

The 1995 estimates also indicate that 56.4 per cent of Sri Lanka's population is concentrated in the south-western part of the island in the eight contiguous administrative districts of Colombo, Gampaha, Kandy, Kurunegala, Kalutara, Galle, Ratnapura and Kegalle, which together constitute only 26.2 per cent of the total land area (annex table B.1). The wet zone and most of the up-country area not only have a dense rural population but also contain the principal conurbation, such as Colombo, Kandy etc. Some of the dry zone districts remain sparsely populated despite considerable colonization since the 1930s.

In Sri Lanka, the pace of urbanization has neither been as spectacular as the rate of population growth nor comparable with the rate of increase of urban population in a large number of developing Asian countries. According to data from the censuses, the proportion of urban population to total population had increased from 15.4 per cent in 1946 to 21.5 per cent in 1981, and currently only about 23 per cent of the population is estimated to be residing in areas nationally defined as urban. The population of Colombo, the capital city, was estimated at 1.9 million in 1990. The slow pace of urbanization could largely be attributed to the fact that the effective implementation of policies that promoted agricultural and rural development also eliminated the massive outflow of population from rural to urban areas. In addition, subsidized transport and a well-developed network of roads and railways have made travel within the country convenient and inexpensive, leading to a kind of rural-urban mobility which does not result in permanent migration.

6. Ethnicity and religion

Sri Lanka is a multi-racial, multi-religious and multi-linguistic country. The majority (74 per cent) of Sri Lankans are Sinhalese, who are deemed to be of Aryan stock and descendents of settlers from north-eastern India. The Sri Lankan Tamils, who account for about 13 per cent of the population, are of Dravidian origin, having descended from the early settlers from south India. The Indian Tamils, who constitute about 6 per cent of the total population, are descendants of those who were brought into the country in the course of the nineteenth and twentieth centuries, mostly to be employed on the plantations. The Sri Lankan Moors are descendants of the Arabs who settled in the country during the eleventh century AD, while the Indian Moors immigrated into the country along with the Indian Tamils. Both these groups together account for about 7 per cent of the country's population. Burghers, who are descendants of the Portugese and the Dutch, and Malays, whose origin is traced to Java, are significant minority groups in the country.

The numerically large Sinhalese are mainly Buddhists, while the majority of the Sri Lankan and Indian Tamils are Hindus. Islam is the religion of the Sri Lankan Moors and the Malays, while Burghers and a small percentage of Sinhalese and Tamils are Christians. According to the 1981 census, 69.3 per cent of Sri Lankans were Buddhists, 15.4 per cent Hindus, 7.6 per cent Muslims, and 7.6 per cent Christians.

Sinhala, a language of Indo-Aryan origin, is the mother tongue of the Sinhalese, while Tamil, which is of Dravidian origin, is the mother tongue of both groups of Tamils and Sri Lankan Moors. English is widely spoken in the country, particularly in business circles. Sinhala, Tamil and English are the official languages.

7. The economy

Sri Lanka, with a per capita GNP estimated at US$ 570 in 1993, continues to be categorized among the developing or low-income economies of the world. Although the country's long-term economic growth rate in per capita terms compares favourably with that of the developing countries in general, this rate is far below that achieved during the past three decades by high-performing economies such as Indonesia, Malaysia, the Republic of Korea and Thailand. The main reason Sri Lanka's economic growth lagging behind the high-performing East Asian economies is that its policies were less supportive of economic growth. Domestic savings and investments were, by and large, constrained by problems with macroeconomic management, which also resulted in galloping inflation. The growth of exports was constrained by inward-looking trade policies, interventions in the labour market and at times by an overvaluation of the exchange rate. Pervasive controls on land ownership and use, marketing and pricing constrained the performance of agriculture, which traditionally constituted the most important sector of the national economy.

The annual growth rate of GDP in real terms had decelerated from 6.1 per cent in 1978-1984 to below 5.0 per cent in 1985-1986 and further, to a little more than 2 per cent, in 1987-1989. However, spurred by renewed stabilization and adjustment efforts, the growth rate jumped to 6.2 per cent in 1990. Since then the rate has been fluctuating, and averaged 5.5 per cent in 1991-1994. A major impediment to Sri Lanka's economic development is the continuing civil war, which consumes about 6 per cent of GDP in defence expenditure.

In recent years, there has been a significant change in the structure of production. Estimates prepared by the Central Bank indicate that the share of the agricultural sector in total output declined gradually from about 26 per cent in 1985 to 20.5 per cent in 1994. During the same period, the relative contribution of the manufacturing sector increased from 14.8 to 19.7 per cent. Indeed, manufacturing has been the star performer of recent years, with increasing participation of the private sector. Banking, insurance and real estate constituted the other buoyant sector, with its relative share increasing from 4.6 per cent in 1985 to 5.5 per cent in 1994 (table 3).

Table 3. Percentage sectoral composition of gross domestic product in real terms (1982 prices): 1985-1994

Sector	1985	1988	1990	1992	1994
Agriculture, forestry and fishing	25.9	23.5	23.2	21.3	20.5
Mining and quarrying	2.2	2.8	3.0	2.3	2.5
Manufacturing	14.8	16.6	17.4	18.5	19.7
Construction	7.4	7.1	6.8	6.9	6.9
Utilities	1.2	1.3	1.3	1.3	1.5
Transport and communications	11.8	11.4	11.1	11.8	11.2
Internal trade	20.9	21.1	20.5	21.3	21.8
Banking, insurance and real estate	4.6	4.9	5.1	5.1	5.5
Ownership of dwellings	3.1	3.0	2.9	2.7	2.4
Public administration and defence	4.0	4.6	4.9	4.6	4.3
Other services	4.0	3.7	3.8	4.1	3.8
GDP at factor cost	100.0	100.0	100.0	100.0	100.0

Source: Central Bank of Sri Lanka, *Annual Report.*

According to the 1994 Labour Force Survey, which did not cover the Northern and Eastern provinces, the agricultural sector accounted for around 42 per cent of local employment, manufacturing for about 14 per cent, and the service sector for 40 per cent. Available data also indicate that unemployment, particularly among the educated youth, has been a persistent problem.

Despite impressive growth in GNP per capita, the income distribution within the country remains skewed. The 1990/91 Household Income and Expenditure Survey revealed that about 30 per cent of the country's households lived in absolute poverty, in that their expenditure on food was insufficient to satisfy their minimum calorie or energy requirements. The incidence of poverty was also reported to be substantially higher in rural areas (34.7 per cent) compared with the urban (18.2 per cent) and estate (20.5 per cent) sectors.

8. Social infrastructure

Sri Lanka has a long history of investment in social development and this early start has resulted in the current social indicators for the country being comparable with those obtaining in countries with income levels much higher than those of Sri Lanka. The government's commitment to the development of social services began during the relatively prosperous years of the late 1940s and the 1950s, when liberal policies were adopted for the expansion and improvement of education and health, and provision of food subsidies, as well as encouraging the building of houses. Since then, successive governments have devoted a sizeable proportion of the national revenue to meeting the basic needs of the people.

(a) Education

Sri Lanka is one of the most educationally advanced countries in the Asian and Pacific region. A system of free education from kindergarten through university was introduced in October 1945, and under this system no tuition fees are charged in government schools, and in universities and technical colleges. Since independence, all national governments have vigorously continued the policy of democratization of educational provision. There has also been a strong drive by the government to provide universal primary education to boys and girls alike. The language of instruction is the pupils' mother tongue, and textbooks are provided free up to grade 8. These and other measures have resulted not only in stimulating unprecedented interest in education throughout the country but also in a rapid expansion in the education system itself. Indeed, the free public education system has become an important source of upward mobility in the society.

The formal education system of Sri Lanka comprises three levels: primary, secondary and tertiary. Primary education begins at 5 years of age and lasts for six years. Secondary schooling starts at 11 years of age and lasts up to seven years, comprising a first cycle of five years and a second cycle of two years. Primary and secondary education is provided through a wide network of schools reaching out to the remotest part of the country. School attendance is officially compulsory for children between 5 and 15 years of age. Tertiary and higher education is provided through technical institutions, colleges and universities.

Data from the Ministry of Education indicate a tremendous expansion in schooling facilities throughout the country. Between 1945 and 1994, the number of schools increased almost twofold, from 5,726 to 10,780, the number of students increased fivefold, from 867,191 to 4,338,329, and the number of teachers expanded more than sevenfold, from 25,581 to 194,979. Since the number of teachers increased faster than the number of students, there has been considerable improvement in the student/teacher ratio; the number of students per teacher declined by almost one third from 33.9 in 1945 to 22.3 in 1994 (table 4). The expansion in school enrolments has also been accompanied by an increase in school participation rates among both boys and girls.

In 1994, there were eight universities located in various parts of the country with a total enrolment of 30,764 students. In addition, there were 30 technical colleges in which over 19,000 students were enrolled for various courses of studies.

(b) Health

The government has, over the past five decades or so, assumed primary responsibility for the health of its people, and the official health policy has aimed at providing basic health services to all citizens so as to enable them to lead socially and economically productive lives. The government has endorsed the goal of "Health for All by the Year 2000" and adopted primary health care (PHC) as the key approach. The country has also succeeded in developing a widespread and generally effective health system at relatively low cost to the consumer. The quality of service provided is impressive for a country of the standard of living of Sri Lanka.

Health-care services are provided through a network of specialized hospitals located in the provincial capitals, district hospitals, rural hospitals, maternity homes, central dispensaries and peripheral units, the last three types constituting the PHC-level institutions. Ordinary out-patient treatment is free in the out-patient departments of all government hospitals and dispensaries, and in-patient medical care is available to all patients free of charge in the

Table 4. Growth of schooling facilities in Sri Lanka: 1945-1994

| Year | Number of | | | Overall student/teacher ratio |
	Schools	Students	Teachers	
1945	5 726	867 191	25 581	33.9
1950	5 487	1 366 742	39 265	34.8
1955	7 011	1 665 796	50 151	33.2
1960	8 046	2 301 568	69 658	33.0
1965	9 550	2 556 191	91 981	27.8
1970	9 931	2 716 187	96 426	28.2
1975	9 675	2 560 479	104 043	24.6
1980	9 794	3 389 776	141 186	24.0
1985	9 914	3 625 897	140 192	25.9
1990	10 382	4 232 356	184 822	22.9
1991	10 520	4 258 697	177 231	24.0
1992	10 586	4 286 275	182 756	23.5
1993	10 713	4 304 897	193 916	22.2
1994	10 780	4 338 329	194 979	22.3

Source: Ministry of Education and Higher Education.

non-paying wards of the government hospitals. In 1991, there were 427 government medical institutions of various types, with a total of 42,437 beds (table 5).

Table 5. Number of government medical institutions and beds: 1991[a/]

Type of institution	Number of	
	Institutions	Beds
Teaching hospitals	10	9 499
Provincial hospitals	6	4 741
Base hospitals	15	5 329
District hospitals	109	11 062
Peripheral units	100	4 512
Rural hospitals	109	2 501
Maternity homes and central dispensaries	62	655
Other institutions	16	4 138
Total	427	42 437

Source: Annual Health Bulletin, Sri Lanka, 1991.

[a/] Excluding medical institutions in Northern and Eastern provinces.

In addition to the public sector, the private sector also plays a significant role in the provision of health-care services in the country. By and large, private medical institutions and personnel are located in the urban areas, where they cater for the health-care needs of those able to pay for the services. Another important feature is the development of the Ayurvedic or indigenous system of medicine along with Western health services. Today both systems of medicine are provided by the government and the private sector.

Besides expanding and strengthening the network of medical institutions, the government has also launched various preventive health programmes, such as the anti-malaria campaign, the BCG campaign to control tuberculosis, the anti-VD campaign, polio immunization, and the expanded programme of immunization for children and infants. The preventive health services also seek to bring about overall development in the quality of life through proper environmental sanitation, reduction in malnutrition and improvement in maternal and child care services.

As a result of the various measures adopted, Sri Lanka has achieved great success in controlling and/or eradicating infectious and contagious diseases and in reducing the incidence of morbidity and mortality. These achievements are reflected in various health indicators. For instance, the present crude death rate is less than half what it was 40 years ago; the 1992 infant mortality rate of 18 per 1,000 live births is comparable with that in a Western European country around the 1960s; maternal mortality is among the lowest in the region; and the life expectancy at birth of 72 years in 1992 is higher than that of any other country in South Asia.

9. Water supply and sanitation

In Sri Lanka, the provision of safe sources of potable water and adequate sanitation (excreta disposal) facilities is deemed to be a critical preventive health measure. Over the years, the government has played a vital role in the provision of these two facilities, and the main objective of official policy has been to achieve complete coverage of the population in both urban and rural areas by 1995.

Although special efforts were made to provide safe water during the International Drinking Water Supply and Sanitation Decade 1981-1990, official estimates indicate that by the end of 1990, only about 67 per cent of the country's population had access to some type of formal[1] water supply facility, this proportion being significantly higher in the urban areas (76 per cent) than in the rural areas (64 per cent). These national averages also conceal the wide variation in coverage among the various provinces; the proportion of total population served varied from a low of 54 per cent in Sabaragamuwa Province to a high of 85 per cent in North-Central Province. The urban coverage was lowest in Eastern (44 per cent) and Northern (49 per cent) provinces, while it was universal in Central Province and

---

[1] A formal source is defined as a piped system for urban areas, and either a piped system, protected open well or handpump for rural areas.

almost universal (94 per cent) in Uva Province (table 6).

It has to be noted, however, that coverage does not necessarily imply provision of service of "satisfactory quality" as, for instance, a 24-hour-a-day supply for piped systems; a functioning handpump supplying water of acceptable taste and quality; or an open well which is provided with an adequate perimeter wall. Estimates made by the National Water Supply and Drainage Board indicate that only 42 per cent of the 11.6 million persons served with some kind of formal water supply in 1990 had access to fully satisfactory service.

Data from the Ministry of Health show that in 1989, only about 59 per cent of the country's population had access to satisfactory sanitation facilities, compared with 48 per cent in 1981. These data also indicate that the percentage of households with latrines varied from a low of 30.3 per cent in Eastern Province and 41.5 per cent in Northern Province to over 65 per cent in Uva, Sabaragamuwa, Southern and Western provinces (table 6).

C. WOMEN'S PROFILE

1. Demographic characteristics

(a) Gender balance

An interesting demographic feature in Sri Lanka is the excess in the number of males over females reported in all 11 censuses held in the country. At the first census held in 1871, females constituted only 46.7 per cent of the total population; in other words, there were then 114.3 males for every 100 females, or 87.5 females for every 100 males in the country. Since then the proportionate share of females in the total population has increased almost continuously and at the last census taken in 1981, females accounted for 49 per cent of the population; there were then 96.2 females for every 100 males, an increase of 8.7 females over the 1871 ratio (table 7).

The reported gender imbalance in the total population has been attributed to the combined effect of several factors, such as a male-favoured sex ratio at birth, higher female

Table 6. Percentage of population covered by water supply and sanitation facilities, by province and area

Province	Water supply 1990			Percentage of households with latrines (all areas) 1989
	Percentage population served in			
	All areas	Urban areas	Rural areas	
Western	72	82	63	76.2
Southern	62	83	58	64.9
Central	70	100	66	71.0
Sabaragamuwa	54	77	52	67.4
North-Western	59	81	58	44.0
North-Central	85	78	86	45.0
Uva	61	94	59	65.0
Northern	68	49	74	41.5
Eastern	63	44	68	30.3
Sri Lanka	67	76	64	59.0

Sources: National Water Supply and Drainage Board, and Ministry of Health, cited in World Bank, *Sri Lanka Poverty Assessment*, Report No. 13431-CE (Washington D.C., January 1995).

Table 7. Enumerated population classified by sex, percentage female and sex ratio:
census years, 1871-1981

| Census year | Enumerated populations | | | | Sex ratio | |
	Both sexes	Male	Female	Percent-age female	Males per 100 females	Females per 100 males
1871	2 400 380	1 280 129	1 120 251	46.7	114.3	87.5
1881	2 759 738	1 469 553	1 290 185	46.8	113.9	87.8
1891	3 007 789	1 593 376	1 414 413	47.0	112.7	88.8
1901	3 565 954	1 896 212	1 669 742	46.8	113.6	88.1
1911	4 106 350	2 175 030	1 931 320	47.0	112.6	88.8
1921	4 498 605	2 381 812	2 116 793	47.1	112.5	88.9
1946	6 657 339	3 532 218	3 125 121	46.9	113.0	88.5
1953	8 097 895	4 268 730	3 829 165	47.3	111.5	89.7
1963	10 582 064	5 498 674	5 083 390	48.0	108.2	92.4
1971	12 689 897	6 531 361	6 158 536	48.5	106.1	94.3
1981	14 846 750	7 568 253	7 278 497	49.0	104.0	96.2

Source: Department of Census and Statistics.

than male mortality, male-predominated immigration, and possible under-enumeration of females at the censuses.

In Sri Lanka, as in most countries the world over, the number of male births exceed the female births every year. Data on registered live births for selected years from 1901 to 1993 indicate that in all years female births accounted for around 49 per cent of total births in the country. Provisional figures for 1993 show that 48.6 per cent of all registered births in that year were female births or that there were 94.4 female births for every 100 male births, or 105.9 male births per 100 female births (table 8).

To some extent, the initial advantage of excess male births tended to be reduced by consistently higher male than female infant

Table 8. Registered live births by sex, percentage of female births and sex ratio at birth:
1901-1993

| Year | Registered births | | | | Sex ratio at birth | |
	Both sexes	Male	Female	Percent-age female	Males per 100 females	Females per 100 males
1901	134 252	68 888	65 364	48.7	105.4	94.9
1911	156 398	79 682	76 716	49.1	103.9	96.3
1921	183 917	93 519	90 398	49.2	103.5	96.7
1931	199 170	101 399	97 771	49.1	103.7	96.4
1941	219 864	112 055	107 809	49.0	103.9	96.2
1951	313 662	159 424	154 238	49.2	103.4	96.7
1961	363 677	184 984	178 693	49.1	103.5	96.6
1971	382 480	195 397	187 083	48.9	104.4	95.7
1981	423 793	217 314	206 479	48.7	105.2	95.0
1991[a]	363 068	185 434	177 634	48.9	104.4	95.8
1992[a]	350 431	178 135	172 296	49.2	103.4	96.7
1993[a]	350 193	180 120	170 073	48.6	105.9	94.4

Source: Registrar General's Department.

[a] Provisional.

mortality rates. However, until the beginning of the 1960s, the higher female mortality at practically all subsequent ages greatly enhanced the balance in favour of males throughout life. During the 1960s, the sex differential in overall mortality began to shift away from a pattern of higher female than male mortality, and equality in the overall level of mortality for the two sexes was observed in the early 1960s. Since then, female mortality rates have been lower than the male rates at all ages excepting the childbearing age groups 15-44 years, and during the past two decades, female rates have been lower than the corresponding male rates at all ages (see table 9). The faster decline in female mortality has been an important factor contributing to the observed increase in the proportionate share of females in the total population in recent decades.

According to recent estimates prepared by the United Nations, the relative share of females in the total population has been increasing further, to 49.5 per cent in 1985, 49.97 per cent in 1990 and 50.3 per cent in 1995. Thus, these estimates indicate that currently females outnumber males in the total population at the rate of about 101.2 females per 100 males. United Nations projections also indicate that this trend will continue in the future, that by 2000 there will be slightly over 102 females per 100 males, and that this ratio will gradually increase to 102.8 in 2010, declining thereafter to 101.7 in 2050 (table 10).

Table 9. Age-specific death rates by gender: 1979 and 1989

(Rates per 1,000 population)

Age group	1979		1989	
	Male	Female	Male	Female
0-4	11.4	10.1	4.4	3.8
5-14	1.0	0.9	0.7	0.6
15-24	2.0	1.7	1.9	1.2
25-34	2.9	2.1	4.9	1.5
35-44	3.9	2.5	7.4	2.3
45-54	8.5	4.7	11.2	4.5
55-64	16.8	11.2	21.3	10.4
65-74	36.1	30.3	44.1	31.0
75 and over	129.3	125.7	114.8	103.7
All ages	7.3	5.7	7.9	4.5

Source: Registrar General's Department, cited in Department of Census and Statistics, *Women and Men in Sri Lanka* (Colombo, May 1995).

Data from the censuses also indicate that, since 1963, the proportionate share of females in Sri Lanka's population has been rising gradually at practically all ages and that this increase has, by and large, been more pronounced in the older age group (table 11) owing to the differential mortality patterns between males and females noted earlier. According to the 1981 census, females almost equalled men at ages 15-49 years and constituted about 96 per cent of the population at ages 0-4 and 5.14 years.

The census data also indicate that while males outnumber females in both urban and

Table 10. Estimated and projected population by sex and sex ratio: 1985-2050

Year	Estimated and projected population (thousands)				Sex ratio	
	Both sexes	Male	Female	Percent-age female	Males per 100 females	Females per 100 males
1985	16 060	8 104	7 956	49.54	101.86	98.17
1990	17 057	8 534	8 523	49.97	100.13	99.87
1995	17 928	8 911	9 017	50.30	98.82	101.19
2000	18 821	9 311	9 510	50.53	97.91	102.14
2010	20 977	10 343	10 633	50.69	97.27	102.80
2020	23 072	11 379	11 693	50.68	97.31	102.76
2030	24 704	12 195	12 509	50.64	97.49	102.57
2040	26 036	12 877	13 160	50.58	97.78	102.27
2050	26 995	13 380	13 614	50.43	98.28	101.75

Source: United Nations, *World Population Prospects: The 1996 Revision* (forthcoming).

Note: Figures for both sexes may not equal the total of males and females in some years because of rounding.

Table 11. Sex ratios by broad age groups: census years of 1953 to 1981

Age group	1953		1963		1971		1981	
	Males per 100 females	Females per 100 males	Males per 100 females	Females per 100 males	Males per 100 females	Females per 100 males	Males per 100 females	Females per 100 males
0-4	101.5	98.4	102.6	97.5	103.0	97.1	103.8	96.4
5-14	104.4	95.8	103.3	96.8	103.4	96.7	103.9	96.3
15-49	115.2	86.8	108.2	92.4	102.2	97.9	102.0	98.0
50-59	135.5	73.8	131.6	76.0	116.2	86.0	111.4	90.3
60+	117.4	85.1	126.3	79.2	121.0	82.7	113.7	87.9
All ages	111.5	89.7	108.2	92.4	104.5	95.6	104.0	96.2

Source: Department of Census and Statistics.

rural areas, the preponderance of males is considerably greater in urban areas. Over the years, however, the relative share of females in the total population has been increasing in both urban and rural areas, but this increase has been more marked in the urban areas (table 12).

(b) Age structure

The numerical as well as percentage distribution of the enumerated population by five-year age group and sex for census years 1953 to 1981 is given in annex tables C.1 and C.2. The distribution of the population by broad age groups as reported in these censuses and in the 1993 Demographic and Health Survey is shown in table 13.

As a result of the changes in the fertility and mortality schedules, there have been significant changes in the age structure of the population of Sri Lanka during the past four decades. The continuing rapid decline in mortality without a compensatory decline in fertility resulted in an increase in the proportionate share of children aged 0-14 years between 1953 and 1963. In 1963, the population was young, in that 40.5 per cent of all males and 42.6 per cent of females were children aged 0-14 years, while another 9.4 per cent of males and 9.9 per cent of females were in the 15-19 age group. Thus, children and youth together then constituted nearly 50 per cent of all males and 52.5 per cent of all females. Since 1963, however, the age structure has been shifting from a young towards an older configuration for both males and females. As a result of the declining fertility, the proportions in the childhood ages have been decreasing and in 1981 only about 35 per cent of males as well as females were below 15 years of age. This proportion declined further to 31.3 per cent for males and 29.4 per cent for females in 1993.

Table 12. Sex ratios by urban and rural residence: census years of 1953 to 1981

Census year	Urban areas			Rural areas		
	Percent-age female	Males per 100 females	Females per 100 males	Percent-age female	Males per 100 females	Females per 100 males
1953	43.28	131.04	76.31	48.01	108.29	92.34
1963	45.88	117.98	84.76	48.54	105.99	94.35
1971	46.87	113.34	88.23	49.01	104.04	96.12
1981	48.46	106.34	94.04	49.47	102.14	97.90

Source: Department of Census and Statistics.

Table 13. Distribution of the population by broad age group and sex: censuses of 1953 to 1981 and Demographic and Health Survey, 1993

Age group	1953 census		1963 census		1971 census		1981 census		1993 DHS	
	Male	Female	Male	Female	Male	Female	Male	Female	Male	Female
0-14	38.3	41.4	40.5	42.6	38.6	39.5	35.2	35.3	31.3	29.4
15-59	56.1	53.5	53.0	51.8	54.0	54.6	57.9	58.4	59.6	61.7
60+	5.6	5.2	6.5	5.6	7.4	5.9	6.9	6.3	9.1	8.9
All ages	100.0	100.0	100.0	100.0	100.0	100.0	100.0	100.0	100.0	100.0
Median age[a]	21.7	19.9	20.0	18.4	20.0	19.3	21.5	21.4	24.0	25.0

Sources: Department of Census and Statistics, reports of censuses for the years 1953-1981; and Sri Lanka Demographic and Health Survey, 1993.

[a] Median age may be defined as the age which divides the population into two equal-sized groups, one of which is younger and the other older than the median.

The decline in the proportion of young children resulted in a concomitant increase in the relative share of persons in working ages 15-59 years between 1953 and 1993. During this 30-year period, the share of the working-age population in the total population rose from 53.0 to 59.6 per cent for males and from 53.8 to 61.7 per cent for females. Thus, the increase in the relative share of the working-age population has been more pronounced in the case of females compared with males. Further, the proportionate share of the elderly, or those aged 60 years and over, also rose, from 5.6 to 9.1 per cent for males and from 5.2 to 8.9 per cent for females between 1953 and 1993, owing to an increase in life expectancy.

Another important change in the age composition of the population has been the steady rise in the proportion of women in the reproductive ages 15-49 years. In 1953, women aged 15-49 years constituted 44.1 per cent of all women, but this proportion increased to 52.1 per cent in 1981 and to 53.0 per cent in 1993. Thus, today more than half the females in Sri Lanka belong to the reproductive age group, with more than a third being concentrated in the peak fertility age, 20-34 years. The high proportion of women in the reproductive age span would mean that, given current patterns of family formation, a substantial addition to the total population would take place over the next

few decades even if fertility rates were to decline further.

The changes in the age structure that had taken place over the year are also reflected in the increase in the median age for both males and females. Until 1981, the median age for females had been slightly lower than that for males but, according to the 1993 Demographic and Health Survey, the female median age is one year higher than that of males (table 13 and figure 3). The 1993 median age of 25 years for females means that exactly half the females were aged 25 years and over and the other half were below 25 years. The

Figure 3. Median age of the population by sex: 1946-1993

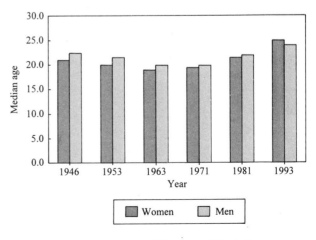

Source: Department of Census and Statistics.

20

relatively higher median age for females could largely be attributed to the longer life expectancy for females compared with males.

(c) Marital status

Although information relating to marital status or conjugal condition was collected at all censuses beginning in 1871, the relevant data collected up to and including the 1921 census have been considered to be subject to errors arising from definition of marriage and its interpretation by the enumerators. However, starting from the 1946 census, problems relating to definitions and concepts were resolved and the data collected on marital status at all subsequent censuses are deemed to be reliable.

The numerical distribution of persons aged 15 years and over by four marital status categories, never-married, married, widowed, and divorced/separated, and by sex is given in annex table C.3, and the percentage distribution is presented in table 14.

It is evident from table 14 that a higher proportion among men than among women aged 15 years and over had remained unmarried or never married in all census years. As will be noted in section D below, the vast majority of the unmarried persons are concentrated in the younger age groups. Data from the censuses also show that, by and large, there was an increase in the proportion never married between 1946 and 1981, but that this increase was more pronounced in the case of women. The proportion of never-married women increased by

11.4 percentage points, from 21.3 per cent in 1946 to 32.4 per cent in 1981, the corresponding increase among men being only 2.7 percentage points. The proportion married among women had declined steadily, from 64.9 per cent in 1953 to 59.0 per cent in 1981; however, in the case of males this proportion declined from 56.7 per cent in 1953 to 53.6 per cent in 1971, but rose again to 55.3 per cent in 1981. As will be discussed in section D, these trends would suggest that there have been significant shifts in marriage patterns in recent decades.

It is also clear from table 14 that the proportion widowed has been declining steadily among both men and women since 1946, but this proportion was considerably higher among women than among men in all the five census years. In 1946, the proportion widowed among women (14.0 per cent) was 3.3 times that (4.2 per cent) reported for men. By 1981, this gender gap had widened, with the proportion widowed among women (8.0 per cent) being 4.4 times that among men (1.8 per cent). The much higher incidence of widowhood among women could be attributed to several factors. As noted earlier, mortality among men is higher than among women, and this, together with the fact that Sri Lankan women generally marry men at least a few years their senior in age, results in a higher incidence of widowhood among women. An equally important reason is that widowers have a better chance of remarriage than widows and thus end their widowhood.

The number of divorced and legally separated persons constituted less than one per

Table 14. Percentage distribution of men and women aged 15 years and over by marital status: censuses of 1946 to 1981

Census year	Men					Women				
	Never married	Married	Widowed	Divorced/ separated	All statuses	Never married	Married	Widowed	Divorced/ separated	All statuses
1946	39.8	55.7	4.2	0.3	100.0	21.3	64.4	14.0	0.3	100.0
1953	38.9	56.7	4.0	0.4	100.0	21.5	64.9	13.1	0.5	100.0
1963	40.7	55.9	3.2	0.2	100.0	26.4	62.9	10.4	0.4	100.0
1971	43.7	53.6	2.3	0.4	100.0	31.3	59.1	9.0	0.6	100.0
1981	42.5	55.3	1.8	0.4	100.0	32.4	59.0	8.0	0.6	100.0

Source: Department of Census and Statistics.

cent among all men and women aged 15 years and over, although this proportion has been slightly higher for women than men as a good proportion of divorced men tend to remarry. In recent decades, an increasing number of divorced women have also been remarrying. Thus, the census data on the divorced population do not give an accurate picture of the incidence of divorce in the country.

2. Educational background

As noted in section B above, the introduction of a system of free education from primary to university and tertiary levels in 1945, and the vigorous pursuit of the policy of democratization of educational provision, as well as the commitment to speedy achievement of the goal of universal primary education by successive national governments, had resulted in a continuous rise in educational participation among both boys and girls in Sri Lanka. Over the years, more and more girls have entered the education system; more have stayed longer in the schools, and more have attained higher educational levels. As will be noted later in this section, Sri Lankan women have been able to achieve educational participation rates and attainment levels that are far superior to those of their counterparts in many developing countries of the world.

A systematic assessment of the progress made in regard to female education in Sri Lanka is also facilitated by the availability of comprehensive and reliable data from various sources on a time series basis. Information on the educational characteristics of the population is available from three independent sources: population censuses, ad hoc sample surveys, and education statistics from the Ministry of Education. The census data on educational characteristics cover school attendance, educational levels completed, and literacy. Several ad hoc sample surveys have also collected information on the educational background of the population surveyed, particularly relating to educational attainment and literacy. The Ministry of Education conducts a school census every year and the information collected includes enrolments by grades and levels, teachers and staff, schools and classrooms etc.

Data from the various sources mentioned above are used to analyse the trends and patterns in educational participation and educational attainment of females and males in the country. It has, however, to be noted that the data from the various sources may not be strictly comparable for several reasons, such as variation in the population covered, the definitions used, and the completeness and accuracy of reporting. Nevertheless, together they give a comprehensive picture of the situation in regard to the education of females vis-à-vis males in the country.

(a) Educational participation

(i) General education

Data from the Ministry of Education indicate that since the beginning of this century, total school enrolments at the primary and secondary levels (grades 1-13) have increased tremendously in respect of both males and females, and that this increase has been more marked in the case of females. Consequently, the relative share of females in total enrolments has risen steadily, from 27.4 per cent in 1901 to 49.8 per cent in 1993 (table 15), thereby reducing the gender differential in formal education to a bare minimum.

Gender disparities in educational enrolments also do not show any significant variation between the nine provinces. In 1993, the relative shares of females in total school enrolments ranged from a low of 48.9 per cent in Eastern Province to a high of 50.6 per cent in Northern Province; this proportion was slightly above 50 per cent in Southern and Sabaragamuwa provinces, while in all other six provinces it was very close to 50 per cent (table 16).

A breakdown of available enrolment data by grades also indicates that while more boys than girls are enrolled in primary-level grades, girls outnumber boys in the higher classes or grades. In 1993, girls constituted 50.5 per cent of total enrolments in grades 6-11, and 57.9 per cent of the enrolments in grades 12-13 (table 17), thus reflecting a higher rate of progression from primary to secondary levels for girls than for boys.

Table 15. Enrolment at primary and secondary levels (grades 1-13) by sex: 1911-1989

Year	Both sexes	Male	Female	Percentage female
1901	183 261	133 086	50 175	27.4
1911	325 282	229 471	95 811	29.5
1921	409 204	274 136	135 068	33.0
1931	593 137	377 080	216 057	36.4
1946	933 358	537 232	396 126	42.4
1953	1 569 360	857 397	711 963	45.4
1963	2 460 694	1 328 407	1 132 287	46.0
1970	2 623 153	1 361 679	1 261 474	48.1
1974	2 596 588	1 336 853	1 259 735	48.5
1978	3 043 629	1 569 366	1 474 263	48.4
1983	3 460 375	1 761 331	1 699 044	49.1
1989	4 643 599	2 340 374	2 303 225	49.6
1993	4 172 897	2 095 615	2 077 282	49.8

Source: Ministry of Education.

Table 16. School enrolment by province and sex: 1985 and 1993

Province	1985			1993		
	Both sexes	Female	Percentage female	Both sexes	Female	Percentage female
Western	858 333	426 060	49.6	905 613	448 187	49.5
Central	476 377	234 249	49.2	571 418	283 662	49.6
Southern	496 324	249 977	50.4	555 336	278 927	50.2
Northern	284 243	142 097	50.0	290 380	147 055	50.6
Eastern	258 262	124 911	48.4	340 006	166 337	48.9
North Western	441 536	220 711	50.0	512 508	254 008	49.6
North Central	233 964	116 264	49.7	281 840	140 510	49.9
Uva	230 020	113 696	49.4	296 703	148 006	49.9
Sabaragamuwa	361 159	182 027	50.4	419 095	210 590	50.2
Sri Lanka	3 640 218	1 809 992	49.7	4 172 899	2 077 282	49.8

Source: Ministry of Education, school censuses of 1985 and 1993.

Table 17. Percentage distribution of enrolment in various grades by sex: selected years, 1970-1993

School grades	1970		1978		1985		1993	
	Male	Female	Male	Female	Male	Female	Male	Female
1-5	53.5	46.5	52.7	47.3	51.8	48.2	51.8	48.2
6-11	50.2	49.8	50.4	49.6	49.1	50.9	49.5	50.5
12-13	49.1	50.5	45.1	54.9	42.2	57.8	42.1	57.9
1-13	51.9	48.1	51.6	48.4	50.3	49.7	50.2	49.8

Source: Ministry of Education, annual school censuses.

There are two important reasons for the relatively lower enrolment of boys at the secondary level of education. According to data from the Ministry of Education, the drop-out rate for boys compared with girls is slightly higher at the primary level and significantly higher at the secondary levels of education. These data also show that in recent years the drop-out rate for girls has been declining but that for boys has shown an increasing trend at the secondary level (table 18 and figure 4). Another important reason is the easier access to employment for boys, even as school drop-outs.

The national average drop-out rates also conceal the marked variations in these rates between the 9 provinces and the 25 constituent districts. Data from the Ministry of Education show that in 1991/92 the drop-out rates up to year 9 in government schools were abnormally high in several districts in Northern and Eastern provinces, owing to the disruption in education caused by the civil war. For instance, the drop-out rate was about 33.0 per cent for both boys and girls in Mannar district, 17.4 per cent for boys and 15.9 per cent for girls in Mullaitivu district, 12.2 per cent for boys and 9.5 per cent for girls in Vavuniya district, and 11.0 per cent for boys and 8.3 per cent for girls in Jaffna district; all these four districts are in Northern Province. In Eastern Province, the drop-out rate was 8.2 per cent for boys and 6.9 per cent for girls in Ampara district. Among other districts not directly affected by the civil

Table 18. Drop-out rates in government schools by educational level and sex: selected years, 1985-1992

Year	Primary level			Secondary level		
	Both sexes	Boys	Girls	Both sexes	Boys	Girls
1985	2.95	3.19	2.69	5.50	6.37	4.63
1987	2.72	2.92	2.50	6.17	7.12	5.19
1990	3.25	3.45	3.03	6.27	7.20	5.30
1991	2.54	2.81	2.46	6.22	7.30	5.12
1992	2.44	2.59	2.28	5.46	6.39	4.51

Source: Ministry of Education.

Figure 4. School drop-out rates at primary and secondary levels of education by sex: selected years, 1985-1992

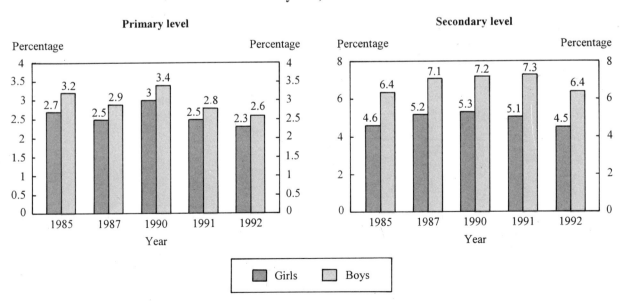

Source: Ministry of Education.

24

war, the female drop-out rate was significantly higher than the national average in Nuwara Eliya, Polonnaruwa and Puttalam districts (annex table C.4).

Another important indicator of the progress made in regard to educational enrolments is the enrolment ratio, or the proportion of children in the eligible or relevant age groups actually enrolled in schools. According to the data from the population censuses of 1963, 1971 and 1981, the enrolment ratio for females was significantly lower than that for males in all age groups in 1963, but by 1981, the age-specific enrolment or participation rate for females was almost equal to that of males at ages 5-14 and slightly higher than the male rates at ages 15-19 and 20-24 years. The 1991 school census data also show an increasing trend in the participation rate for boys and girls at ages 5-14, but at ages 5-19 there was a decline in the rate for boys from 41.2 per cent in 1981 to 37.5 per cent in 1991, while the rate for girls remained almost unchanged at 42.7 per cent. However, data from the population as well as the school censuses confirm the earlier findings that more girls than boys are enrolled in the secondary schools (table 19).

A further analysis of the 1981 population census data indicates that there are significant differences in female age-specific participation rates between urban and rural areas. The urban female rate exceeds the rural female rate by 3.2 percentage points at ages 5-14 years and by 1.5 percentage points at ages 20-24 years, but this difference is more marked at ages 15-19 years, where the urban rate is 6.7 percentage points higher than the rural female rate. It may also be noted from table 20 that the female participation rate is higher than the rate for males at ages 15-19 years in both rural and urban areas, while at ages 20-24 years the female rate is slightly higher than the male

Table 19. Age-specific enrolment rates in schools by sex: population censuses of 1963 to 1981 and school census of 1991

Age group	1963			1971			1981			1991		
	Both sexes	Boys	Girls	Both sexes	Boys	Girls	Both sexes	Boys	Girls	Both sexes	Boys	Girls
5-14	74.4	76.7	72.0	65.3	66.8	63.7	83.7	83.7	83.6	87.9	85.3	87.4
15-19	40.0	43.3	36.6	35.0	37.1	32.9	41.9	41.2	42.7	39.9	37.5	42.6
20-24	4.4	5.3	4.0	7.4	8.1	7.0	8.9	8.7	9.0	3.8[a]	3.1[a]	4.9[a]
5-24	53.8	56.2	51.3	46.0	47.6	44.0	55.8	56.0	55.6	62.8[b]	62.1[b]	63.4[a]

Sources: Department of Census and Statistics, population censuses of 1963, 1971 and 1981; and Ministry of Education, school census of 1991.

[a] Referring to ages 20-22 years.
[b] Referring to ages 5-22 years.

Table 20. Age-specific school enrolment rates by urban and rural areas and sex: 1981 population census

Age group	Urban			Rural		
	Both sexes	Male	Female	Both sexes	Male	Female
5-14	85.9	86.4	85.6	82.7	83.1	82.4
15-19	46.7	44.9	48.0	40.6	40.0	41.3
20-24	9.7	9.4	10.2	8.7	9.1	8.7
5-24	56.6	55.3	57.3	55.7	56.3	55.1

Source: Department of Census and Statistics, population census of 1981.

rate in urban areas and lower than the male rate in rural areas.

It is also evident from the data presented in table 19 that, despite nearly five decades of positive and vigorous educational policies, Sri Lanka has not been able to achieve universal primary education. Currently, over 10 per cent of children in the eligible age cohort (5-14 years) remain outside the school system. Various surveys and studies have revealed that the plantation districts of Nuwara Eliya and Badulla, as well as the districts of Moneragala, Ampara, Batticaloa and Trincomalee in the eastern hinterlands, including concentrations of Muslim villages, have remained educationally disadvantaged for a long time. Gender disparities in participation rates among the 5-14 age group are also wide in these districts and are particularly pronounced among two population groups: Muslims in eastern coastal districts, and the resident plantation labour of Indian origin in Badulla and Nuwara Eliya districts.

Although equal opportunities exist for boys and girls at higher secondary levels, there appears to be a stereotyping in the selection of subject streams. Data from the Ministry of Education showed that in 1992 girls were concentrated in the arts and commerce courses, while boys accounted for about 55 per cent of enrolments in the economically more rewarding science courses (table 21).

Various studies have shown conclusively that there are hardly any gender differences in abilities in the entry-level competence of 5-year-old children in language and social skills, as well as in regard to the general ability of pupils in secondary-level education. Data from the Ministry of Education have also shown that repetition rates in school grades have consistently been higher for boys than for girls: 10.1 per cent for boys and 8.2 per cent for girls in 1984, and 9.3 per cent for boys and 8.2 per cent for girls in 1992.

Data from the Examinations Department also reveal that girls outnumbered boys at public examinations; 53 per cent of total candidates appearing for the General Certificate of Education Ordinary Level Examination in 1994 were girls, and girls also constituted 56 per cent of total candidates appearing for the General Certificate of Education Advanced Level Examination in that year. In general, girls performed better than boys at both these examinations (figure 5). Available data indicate that at the 1994 GCE Ordinary Level Examination, 21.7 per cent of the girls who appeared passed in six or more subjects with at least three credits, the corresponding proportion for boys being 19.7 per cent. At the GCE Advanced Level Examination of 1994, 46.3 per cent of female candidates and 43.1 per cent of male candidates qualified for university admission.

The progress made in regard to female education in Sri Lanka could be attributed to a combination of several factors. In the first instance, as noted in section B above, the provision of tuition-free public education, free textbooks and, in recent years, free school uniforms to all children irrespective of race, religion and

Table 21. Enrolment in grades 12 and 13 by field of study and sex: 1992

Grade and field of study	Both sexes	Male	Female	Percentage female	Females per 100 males
Grade 12					
Science	18 392	10 254	8 138	44.2	79.4
Commerce	22 950	11 567	11 383	49.6	98.4
Arts	38 191	12 565	25 626	67.1	203.9
Grade 13					
Science	17 781	9 771	8 010	45.0	82.0
Commerce	20 472	9 827	10 645	52.0	108.3
Arts	30 056	8 941	21 115	70.3	236.2

Source: Ministry of Education, *Education Statistics of Sri Lanka, 1992.*

Figure 5. Performance at the General Certificate of Education Ordinary Level and General Certificate of Education Advanced Level Examinations, by sex: 1994

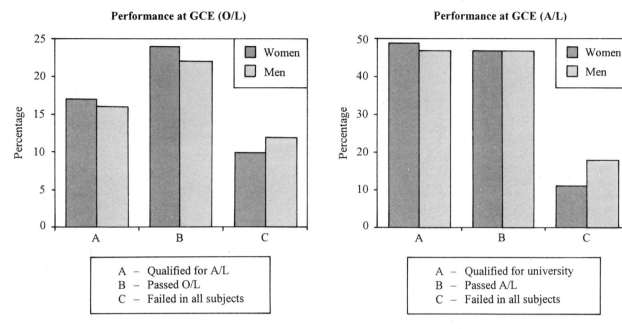

Performance at GCE (O/L)

Performance at GCE (A/L)

A – Qualified for A/L
B – Passed O/L
C – Failed in all subjects

A – Qualified for university
B – Passed A/L
C – Failed in all subjects

Source: Department of Examinations.

gender, together with the provision of educational facilities within easy access of the students, had been largely instrumental in an increasing number of boys as well as girls attending the schools. Second, the link between education and upward socio-economic mobility established during the colonial period raised the level of parental aspirations for the education of their children. The perception of parents that the education of their children would help to enhance family income and status accounts for the fact that most Sri Lankan parents, even from the lowest social strata, have equally high educational aspirations for their sons and daughters. Third, as revealed by several studies, son preference is not as marked in Sri Lanka as it is in most South and South-East Asian countries so as to hinder the participation of girls in the education system.

(ii) Technical and vocational education

A systematic and comprehensive analysis of gender participation in technical and vocation education is rendered difficult by two factors: the lack of a complete inventory of vocational and technical training institutions in the country, and the non-availability at times of relevant gender-disaggregated data and information. Nevertheless, available data suggest that gender disparity in participation is widest and gender-role stereotyping is more marked in the technical-vocation subsector of the national education system.

Student enrolments in 26 technical colleges by course of study and by gender in 1984 and 1992 are shown in table 22. It will be noted that the proportionate share of women in total enrolments increased significantly, from 37.2 per cent in 1984 to 40.7 per cent in 1992. However, the vast majority of female students are enrolled in courses such as English, stenography, business, accounting, home economics/home science etc., while male students are largely concentrated in technology and crafts courses. In 1984, women accounted for 70-100 per cent of students enrolled in courses for occupations in the service sector, such as business studies, languages, and secretarial work, and for occupations in the garment industry, such as tailoring; only about 15 per cent of enrolments in technical courses were women.

Available data also indicate that the gender imbalance in enrolments is even more marked in respect of other vocational training programmes. For instance, in 1986, nearly 70 per

Table 22. Enrolment in technical colleges by course of study and sex: 1984

Study course	1984			1992		
	Both sexes	Female	Percentage female	Both sexes	Female	Percentage female
Diploma in technology	817	155	19.0	205	52	25.4
Diploma in jewellery design and manufacture	–	–	–	22	8	36.4
Certificate in technology	4 033	370	9.2	2 634	396	15.0
Trades/crafts	2 289	151	6.6	2 583	158	6.1
Diploma in agriculture	196	43	21.9	201	49	24.4
Certificate in agriculture	–	–	–	62	25	40.3
Diploma in accountancy/commerce	4 553	1 988	43.7	2 953	1 538	52.1
Diploma in business studies	–	–	–	483	299	61.9
Certificate in business studies	3 894	2 760	70.9	772	557	72.2
Accounting technicians	–	–	–	1 582	972	61.4
Stenography	–	–	–	1 517	1 375	90.6
Quantity surveying	–	–	–	661	324	49.0
Draughtsmanship	661	348	52.6	662	358	54.1
Construction trades	–	–	–	1 852	4	0.2
Diploma in home economics/science	113	113	100.0	151	151	100.0
Tailoring	82	39	47.6	88	73	83.0
Diploma in English	–	–	–	330	238	72.1
Certificate in English	1 403	737	52.5	1 310	778	59.4
All courses	18 041	6 704	37.2	18 068	7 355	40.7

Source: Technical Education Branch, Ministry of Higher Education, cited in Centre for Women's Research, *Facets of Change: Women in Sri Lanka, 1986-1995* (Colombo, July 1995).

cent of all trainees enrolled in the non-formal technical units organized by the Ministry of Education for all school-leavers and drop-outs were females, but while nearly 90 per cent of all female trainees were in dressmaking courses, male trainees were predominantly enrolled in motor mechanism, air-conditioning and refrigeration, electric wiring, woodwork and metalwork courses. This pattern has continued; in 1991, females constituted about 74 per cent of the total enrolments and 90 per cent of female trainees were in dressmaking courses.

The relative share of women in total enrolments in the vocational training centres of the Department of Labour increased from 29.2 per cent in 1977 to 77.3 per cent in 1982, but declined thereafter to 56.4 per cent in 1987 and 30.2 per cent in 1994. Available data also indicate that nearly 95 per cent of women enrollees in all these years were in sewing and industrial sewing courses.

According to data from the National Apprenticeship and Industrial Training Authority, in 1992 women constituted about 52 per cent of trainees in various courses under the craft apprenticeship scheme, and 62 per cent of trainees in village-level apprenticeship courses. However, the vast majority of women trainees were enrolled in courses for the textile and garment industry trades, services, and the clerical and allied trades, and were either not represented or very much underrepresented in the automobile, building and electrical trades (annex table C.5).

It is thus clear from the foregoing analysis that while the number of females enrolled for various vocational and technical courses has increased substantially over the years, women still have limited access to the technical skills that are in increasing demand in an industrializing economy.

(iii) Higher education

The increasing participation as well as remarkable performance of girls in upper secondary education has resulted in an increasing number of women being admitted to the universities over the years. Data from the

University Grants Commission indicate that the relative share of females in total university enrolments had increased dramatically from 10.1 per cent in 1942/43 to 44.4 per cent in 1970/71 and more or less stabilized at this level thereafter, with minor fluctuations (table 23).

Perhaps what is more significant about the rapid rise in university enrolments is the fact that over the years there have been radical changes in the socio-economic background of the students admitted to the various universities in the country. Studies relating to the parental occupation of university entrants indicate that whereas in 1950 about 88 per cent of male and 97 per cent of female entrants came from high- and middle-income groups, in 1977 these income groups accounted for only 34 per cent of the male and 36 per cent of the female students entering university. In other words, by 1977, the socio-economic composition of the university entrants had changed very significantly, with a majority of the students (56 per cent males and 51 per cent females) belonging to families in which parents were either workers or were unemployed (table 24).

Although the enrolment of women students in the undergraduate faculties of the various universities has been increasing in absolute as well as relative terms over the years, gender stereotyping in regard to the selection of subject courses persists, resulting in imbalances in enrolments between the two sexes in various courses of studies. It could be estimated from annex table C.6 that, in all four academic years for which data have been presented, a higher proportion among women than among men students has been enrolled in arts-based study courses, while the proportion enrolled in science and science-based professional courses has been higher among males than among females. There have, however, been changes in these proportions over the years with, for example, the proportion among females enrolled in science and science-based professional courses increasing threefold from 13.4 per cent in

Table 24. Percentage distribution of university entrants by sex and parents' occupation: 1950 and 1977

Parents' occupation	1950		1977	
	Male	Female	Male	Female
Professional and management	55.5	69.5	8.9	11.3
Teaching	12.6	7.2	9.8	10.5
Middle-level clerical	20.3	20.3	15.3	14.3
Rural workers	6.3	1.4	31.5	27.9
Urban workers	4.2	1.4	16.2	15.0
Unemployed	–	–	8.3	8.5
Unspecified	1.1	0.2	10.0	12.5
Total	100.0	100.0	100.0	100.0

Sources: Murray Strans, "Family characteristics and occupational choice of university entrants", *University of Ceylon Review*, vol. 9, No. 2, April 1957; and Swarna Jayaweera, "Access to university education: the social composition of university entrants", *University of Colombo Review*, 1984.

Table 23. Student enrolment in universities by sex: 1942/43 to 1991/92

Year	Both sexes	Male	Female	Percentage female
1942/43	904	813	91	10.1
1945/46	1 065	932	133	12.5
1950/51	2 036	1 655	381	18.7
1955/56	2 431	1 781	650	26.7
1960/61	4 723	3 587	1 136	24.1
1965/66	14 210	9 631	4 579	32.2
1970/71	11 813	6 570	5 243	44.4
1975/76	12 648	7 496	5 152	40.7
1980/81	17 494	10 544	6 950	39.7
1985/86	18 903	10 743	8 160	43.2
1988/89	24 666	14 134	10 532	42.7
1990/91	28 363	16 232	12 131	42.8
1991/92	30 637	17 045	13 592	44.4

Source: University Grants Commission.

1966/67 to 40.2 per cent in 1991/92. Yet in 1991/92, the majority of women students (59.8 per cent) were enrolled in arts-based courses, while the majority of male students (55.6 per cent) were enrolled in science and science-based professional courses.

Nevertheless, during the past 25 years or so, women have made considerable headway in entering those fields of studies which have traditionally been dominated by men. Between 1966/67 and 1991/92, the relative share of women in total enrolments increased from 28.8 to 43.0 per cent in the medical faculty; from 37.9 to 52.1 per cent in dentistry; from 14.3 to 44.1 per cent in veterinary sciences; from 13.3 to 44.6 per cent in agriculture; and from 24.6 to 41.6 per cent in the science facuties. While women account for 47.4 per cent of enrolments in architecture courses, they are very much underrepresented in the engineering courses, constituting only 12.2 per cent of the enrolments in 1991/92. Females outnumber males in enrolments in dentistry, law and social sciences and humanities, and in 1991/92 they constituted about 42 per cent of all students enrolled in arts-based courses (table 25).

Although, as noted earlier, the number of women enrolled in various faculties of the universities has, by and large, been increasing over the years, available data indicate that there has been a decrease in the overall share of women in the total number of students graduating, from 47.0 per cent in 1985 to 43.6 per cent in 1990, but the pattern varies from one faculty to another. For instance, the number of females graduating from the medical faculty declined from 169 in 1985 to 122 in 1990, and their relative share in the total number of medical graduates also declined, from 50.0 to 38.9 per cent, during the same period. Similarly, the number of women graduates, as well as their relative share in the total number graduating in science, also recorded a decline during the five-year period. But the number of women graduating in agriculture, management studies and commerce and their respective relative proportions increased between 1985 and 1990 (table 26).

Women also constitute a very significant proportion (36 per cent in 1991/92) of students enrolled in various postgraduate-level courses at the universities in Sri Lanka, and their number

Table 25. Percentage share of women students in total undergraduate enrolment in universities by faculty: selected years, 1966/67 to 1991/92

Faculty	1966/67	1975/76	1985/86	1991/92
Medicine	28.8	47.1	42.9	43.0
Dentistry	37.9	56.0	55.7	52.1
Veterinary science	14.3	49.1	42.9	44.1
Agriculture	13.3	25.6	36.0	44.6
Engineering	1.9	10.4	15.0	12.2
Architecture	–	28.8	45.4	47.4
Science	24.6	36.7	41.8	41.6
Management studies	–	29.6	42.4	44.1
Law	–	63.1	47.5	56.9
Social sciences and humanities[a]	41.8	42.4	51.9	55.9
Total	**37.3**	**40.7**	**43.2**	**44.4**
Total professional science courses[b]	21.4	30.9	33.6	33.6
Total science courses[c]	24.6	36.7	41.8	41.6
Total arts-based courses[d]	41.7	45.8	48.6	51.8

Sources: Kumari Jayawardena and Swarna Jayaweera, "The integration of women in development planning: Sri Lanka", in Noeleen Heyzer, ed., *Missing Women: Development Planning in Asia and the Pacific* (Kuala Lumpur, Asian and Pacific Development Centre); and Swarna Jayaweera, "Women and education" in Centre for Women's Research, *Facets of Change: Women in Sri Lanka, 1985-1995* (Colombo, July 1995).

[a] Including education.

[b] Comprising medicine, dentistry, veterinary science, agriculture, engineering and architecture.

[c] Comprising science.

[d] Comprising management studies, law social sciences and humanities.

Table 26. Output of graduates from universities by field of study and sex: 1985 and 1990

Field of study	1985				1990			
	Both sexes	Male	Female	Percent-age female	Both sexes	Male	Female	Percent-age female
Medicine	338	169	169	50.0	314	192	122	38.9
Dentistry	45	25	20	44.4	27	14	13	48.1
Veterinary science	24	12	12	50.0	34	22	12	35.3
Agriculture	162	112	50	30.9	175	112	63	36.0
Engineering	247	201	46	18.6	454	373	81	17.8
Architecture	42	28	14	33.3	39	26	13	33.3
Science	831	457	374	45.0	814	472	342	42.0
Management studies	261	167	94	36.0	293	184	109	37.2
Law	64	30	34	53.1	88	45	43	48.9
Commerce	480	277	203	42.3	479	240	239	49.9
Arts	1 987	897	1 090	54.9	1 759	844	915	52.0
Total	4 481	2 375	2 106	47.0	4 476	2 524	1 952	43.6

Source: University Grants Commission, cited in Women's Affairs Division, Ministry of Transport, Environment and Women's Affairs, *Towards Gender-Equity: The Sri Lanka National Report to the (1995) Fourth United Nations World Conference on Women* (Colombo, November 1994).

as well as relative share in total enrolments in respect of some study courses has been increasing in recent years. Although there was a dramatic increase in the number of males as well as females enrolled for postgraduate diploma courses between 1988/89 and 1991/92, this increase was more marked in the case of females, whose share in enrolments for this course increased from 39.5 to 47.6 per cent during the three-year period. There have also been significant increases in the proportionate share of women enrolled for M. Phil. and Ph. D. courses at the universities (table 27).

In addition to the eight universities, higher and tertiary-level education is also provided by several postgraduate and undergraduate institutions in specific fields, by affiliated university colleges, and the open university. The data on enrolments in postgraduate and undergraduate institutions presented in table 28 show that in general there was an increase in the number of females enrolled in these institutions between 1985 and 1994. At the Postgraduate Institute of Medicine, although the enrolment of females more than doubled from 100 to 255, their relative share in total enrolments remained

Table 27. Enrolment of postgraduate students in universities by course of study and sex: 1988/89 and 1991/92

Study course	1988/89				1991/92			
	Both sexes	Male	Female	Percent-age female	Both sexes	Male	Female	Percent-age female
Postgraduate diploma	248	150	98	39.5	1 262	661	601	47.6
M.A./M.Sc.	747	459	288	38.6	778	515	263	33.8
M. Phil.	171	112	59	34.5	283	177	106	37.4
Ph. D.	131	94	37	28.2	141	93	48	34.0
Other	927	559	368	39.7	719	584	135	18.8
Total	2 224	1 374	850	38.2	3 183	2 030	1 153	36.2

Source: Ministry of Education and Higher Education.

Table 28. Student enrolment in postgraduate and undergraduate institutions, by sex: 1985 and 1994

Institution	1985			1994		
	Both sexes	Female	Percentage female	Both sexes	Female	Percentage female
Postgraduate Institute of Medicine	269	100	37.2	687	255	37.1
Postgraduate Institute of Agriculture	195	52	26.7	310	84	27.1
Postgraduate Institute of Management	103	6	5.8	287	38	13.2
Postgraduate Institute of Archaeology	32	6	18.8	150	39	26.0
Postgraduate Institute of Pali and Buddhist Studies	83	6	7.2	412	50	12.1
Institute of Computer Technology	–	–	–	117	27	23.1
Institute of Aesthetic Technology	515	398	77.3	1 049	846	80.6
Institute of Indigenous Studies	241	148	61.4	359	218	60.7
Institute of Workers Education	467	88	18.8	428	125	29.2

Source: University Grants Commission.

more or less unchanged, at about 37 per cent. In the Institute of Aesthetic Studies, females not only outnumber males by a wide margin but have also increased their proportionate share from 77.2 to 80.6 per cent. Between 1985 and 1994, female enrolments increased in absolute and relative terms at the Postgraduate Institution of Archaeology, the Postgraduate Institution of Pali and Buddhist Studies and the Institute of Workers Education, but at the Institute of Indigenous Studies, while their numbers increased from 148 to 218, their relative share declined slightly, from 61.4 to 60.7 per cent.

In 1994, women accounted for 62 per cent of the 2,276 students enrolled in the various affiliated university colleges. More than a third (35.1 per cent) of the 1,417 women students were enrolled for the course in English while about another quarter (24.7 per cent) were enrolled in accountancy and finance. Females also outnumbered males in almost all courses of study excepting travel and tourism, hotel management and agriculture (table 29).

Although the total number of women enrolled in various courses of study at the Open

Table 29. Enrolment in affliated university colleges by study course and sex: 1994

Course of study	Both sexes		Male		Female		Percentage female
	Number	Percentage	Number	Percentage	Number	Percentage	
English	725	31.9	228	26.5	497	35.1	68.6
Accountancy and finance	654	28.7	304	35.4	350	24.7	53.5
Travel and tourism	63	2.8	34	4.0	29	2.0	46.0
Hotel management	42	1.8	27	3.1	15	1.0	35.7
Entrepreneurship and small business management	255	11.2	98	11.4	157	11.1	61.6
Agriculture	222	9.8	115	13.4	107	7.6	48.2
Home science	177	7.8	8	0.9	169	11.9	95.5
Mathematical science	31	1.4	9	1.0	22	1.6	71.0
Tourism and culture	57	2.5	19	2.2	38	2.7	66.7
Bio-science (special)	50	2.2	17	2.0	33	2.3	66.0
Total	2 276	100.0	859	100.0	1 417	100.0	62.3

Source: University Grants Commission.

University increased from 5,250 in 1988/89 to 5,563 in 1990/91, their relative proportion declined significantly, from 44.6 to 36.0 per cent during these two years, indicating that more men than women have been availing themselves of the learning opportunities provided by the Open University. In 1990/91, females outnumbered males in several certificate-level courses and in pre-school education, professional English, and textile technology, as well as in the bachelor degree course in science and the postgraduate-level course in education. But females were very much underrepresented in the two technology courses and in the certificate courses in journalism and sociology (table 30).

(iv) Teaching profession

An important factor responsible for the rapid expansion of female enrolments in primary and secondary schools may be the availability in adequate numbers of female teachers. On account of the high literacy levels attained by women over the past six decades and their

preference for the teaching profession, an increasing number have been recruited into the teaching service annually. Consequently, available data indicate that today females outnumber males among teachers at the primary and secondary schools. The proportionate share of women in the total number of primary- and secondary-level teachers increased from 61.2 per cent in 1985 to 67.2 per cent in 1993 (table 31).

Although the relative share of women teachers increased significantly between 1985 and 1993, this increase has largely been due to a rise in the number of less qualified women teachers. The proportion of women teachers who are professionally trained (trained + nongraduate diploma) actually declined, from about 57 per cent in 1985 to 45 per cent in 1993. Further, although women constitute a substantially higher proportion of primary and secondary schoolteachers, they are more likely to remain teachers throughout their career because, compared with males, only very few females have been appointed as principals in the Sri Lanka Educational Administrative

Table 30. Student enrolment at the Open University by course of study and sex: 1988/89 and 1990/91

Course of study	1988/89				1990/91			
	Both sexes	Male	Female	Percentage female	Both sexes	Male	Female	Percentage female
Certificate in								
Entrepreneurship and small business	346	292	54	15.6	554	422	132	23.8
Journalism	–	–	–	–	196	162	34	17.3
Pre-school education	238	–	238	100.0	554	1	553	99.8
Professional English	2 187	1 034	1 153	52.7	2 342	1 089	1 253	53.5
Sociology	–	–	–	–	123	86	37	30.1
Textile technology	74	42	32	43.2	84	33	51	60.7
Diploma in								
Management	733	610	123	16.8	2 855	2 187	668	23.4
Technology	1 691	1 420	271	16.0	3 159	2 748	411	13.0
Bachelor degree in								
Law	1 705	1 240	465	27.3	1 806	1 338	468	25.9
Science	2 089	1 044	1 045	50.0	2 413	1 204	1 209	50.1
Technology	51	48	3	5.9	213	190	23	10.8
Postgraduate degree in								
Education	2 654	788	1 866	70.3	1 154	430	724	62.7
Total	11 768	6 518	5 250	44.6	15 453	9 890	5 563	36.0

Source: University Grants Commission.

Table 31. Teachers by qualifications and sex: 1985 and 1993

Qualification	1985				1993			
	Both sexes	Male	Female	Percent-age female	Both sexes	Male	Female	Percent-age female
Graduates	28 507	12 429	16 078	56.4	46 968	18 306	28 662	61.0
Non-graduate diploma	230	106	124	53.9	3 986	1 539	2 447	61.4
Trained	82 380	32 817	49 563	60.2	79 690	26 460	53 230	66.8
Certificated	7 741	2 708	5 033	65.0	4 926	1 626	3 300	67.0
Uncertificated	21 338	6 163	15 175	71.1	12 439	4 044	8 395	67.5
Other	2 044	971	1 073	52.5	38 917	9 426	29 491	75.8
Total	142 240	55 194	87 046	61.2	186 926	61 401	125 525	67.2

Source: Ministry of Education, school censuses of 1985 and 1993.

Service. Available data indicate that in 1993 women constituted 46 per cent of principals in class I, 21.5 per cent in class II and 23.8 per cent in class III.

At the universities, women constitute less than a third of the academic staff, and are mostly employed at the lower grades. Of the 598 female academic staff employed in 1991, about 59 per cent were in the lecturer and assistant lecturer grades; at these levels, women constituted about 38 per cent of the total 932 staff members. But at higher levels women were grossly underrepresented, constituting about 8 per cent of all professors, 20 per cent of associate professors and 24 per cent of grade I senior lecturers (table 32).

(b) Educational attainment

Consequent upon the continuously rising participation of women in the education system, there has been a steady increase in the level of their educational attainment as measured in terms of the proportion completing particular educational level or cycles, as well as in terms of overall literacy rates.

(i) Educational level

Data on the educational level of persons aged 10 years and over obtained through the population censuses of 1963, 1971 and 1981, as well as through the 1985/86 Labour Force and Socio-economic Survey and the 1990/91 Household Income and Expenditure Survey, are presented in table 33.

It will be noted from table 33 that, according to the data from the three population censuses, the proportion of women with no schooling (or who have never attended school) had almost halved, from 33.8 per cent in 1963 to 17.5 per cent in 1981, while that of females with some primary education had more than halved, from 28.2 to 11.4 per cent during the

Table 32. Academic staff of the universities by level and sex: 1991

Staff level	Both sexes	Male	Female	Percentage female
Professor	184	170	14	7.6
Associate professor	96	77	19	19.8
Senior lecturer I	340	259	81	23.8
Senior lecturer II	361	228	133	36.8
Lecturer/assistant lecturer	932	581	351	37.7
Total	1 913	1 315	598	31.3

Source: University Grants Commission.

Table 33. Percentage distribution of persons aged 10 years and over by level of education completed and sex: censuses of 1963 to 1981 and sample surveys of 1985/86 and 1990/91

Education level	1963		1971		1981		1985/86		1990/91	
	Male	Female	Male	Female	Male	Female	Male	Female	Male	Female
No schooling	15.7	33.8	16.0	29.5	8.7	17.5	8.8	15.6	6.1	11.3
Incomplete primary	33.9	28.2	26.9	22.7	13.6	11.4	36.4	33.3	35.4	32.5
Completed primary or incomplete secondary	42.5	31.6	50.7	42.4	68.2	62.3	41.1	37.0	42.2	38.4
Secondary GCE (Ordinary Level)	6.5	5.5	4.5	4.5	7.0	7.0	11.0	11.0	12.6	13.2
Secondary GCE (Advanced Level)	1.4	0.9	1.2	0.9	1.4	1.4	2.0	2.5	3.0	4.1
University degree or higher	–	–	0.6	0.1	0.9	0.5	0.9	0.6	0.7	0.5
Total	100.0	100.0	100.0	100.0	100.0	100.0	100.0	100.0	100.0	100.0

Sources: Department of Census and Statistics, population censuses of 1963, 1971 and 1981; Labour Force and Socio-economic Survey, 1985/86; and Household Income and Expenditure Survey, 1990/91.

same period. Consequently, the proportion of women who had completed primary education or had some secondary education almost doubled, from 31.6 per cent in 1963 to 62.3 per cent in 1981. However, according to the sample surveys conducted in 1985/86 and 1990/91, while the proportion who never attended school had declined further during the 1980s, the proportion with incomplete primary education (or those who attended school but could not complete the primary level of education) had increased sharply, and in 1990/91 about 33 per cent of females and 35 per cent of males were reported to have not completed primary education. The proportion of women who had had at least 10 years of schooling (General Certificate of Education (Ordinary Level and above)) had been increasing, from 6.4 per cent in 1963 to 8.9 per cent in 1981 and further to 17.8 per cent in 1990/91.

The educational levels of the population aged 10 years and over vary between the urban, rural and estate sectors of the country. Data from the 1985/86 Labour Force and Socio-economic Survey revealed that among women, the proportion with no schooling ranged from a low of 10.5 per cent in urban areas to 14.9 per cent in rural areas and to 43.8 per cent in the estate sector. In other words, the percentage of women who had never attended

school in the estate areas was more than four times the percentage for urban women and about three times that among rural women. Only about 14 per cent of estate women compared with about 42 per cent of urban and 37 per cent of rural women had completed primary education or had had some secondary education. Further, while 19.3 per cent of urban women had at least 10 years of schooling, the corresponding proportion was 13.3 per cent for rural women and only 3.4 per cent for estate women (table 34).

(ii) Literacy rates

Information regarding the literacy of persons aged 10 years and over has been collected at the various censuses held in the country beginning from the second census held in 1881. For census purposes, a literate person was one who could both read and write any language. Similar information was collected by the 1986/87 Survey of Demographic and Social Aspects and the 1990/91 Household Income and Expenditure Survey. The literacy rates as reported by the censuses and surveys are shown in table 35.

It is evident from table 35 that the literacy rate for both males and females aged 10 years and over had been rising continuously over the years but that the progress made in regard to

Table 34. Percentage distribution of persons aged 10 years and over by educational level, sector and sex: 1985/86

Educational level	Urban		Rural		Estate	
	Male	Female	Male	Female	Male	Female
No schooling	6.3	10.5	8.5	14.9	19.9	43.8
Incomplete primary	27.4	28.3	38.1	34.4	48.5	38.7
Completed primary or incomplete secondary	45.5	41.9	40.8	37.4	27.1	14.1
Secondary GCE (Ordinary Level)	15.5	14.1	10.2	10.7	4.2	2.6
Secondary GCE (Advanced Level)	3.3	4.0	1.8	2.1	0.3	0.7
University degree or higher	2.0	1.2	0.6	0.5	–	0.1
Total	100.0	100.0	100.0	100.0	100.0	100.0

Source: Department of Census and Statistics, *Labour Force and Socio-economic Survey, 1985/86.*

female literacy has been remarkable. At the turn of the century, the female literacy rate was only 8.5 per cent, or about a fifth of that for males. But in the course of the subsequent eight decades, the literacy rate increased about tenfold to 83.2 per cent in 1981. Consequently, the gap between the male and female literacy rates had been narrowing steadily, from 33.5 percentage points in 1901 to 7.9 percentage points in 1981. Data from various sample surveys conducted since 1981 suggest that there

Table 35. Percentage of literate persons aged 10 years and over by sex: 1901-1991

Year	Both sexes	Male	Female	Male/ female difference
1901	26.4	42.0	8.5	33.5
1911	31.0	47.2	12.5	34.7
1921	39.9	56.4	21.2	35.2
1946	57.8	70.1	43.8	26.3
1953	65.4	75.9	53.6	22.3
1963	71.6	79.3	63.2	16.1
1971	78.5	85.6	70.9	14.7
1981	87.2	91.1	83.2	7.9
1985/86	84.2	88.6	80.0	8.6
1986/87	89.3	93.7	87.7	6.0
1990/91	86.9	90.0	83.8	6.2

Sources: 1901 to 1981: Population censuses.
1985/86: Labour Force and Socio-economic Survey.
1986/87: Consumer Finance and Socio-economic Survey.
1990/91: Household Income and Expenditure Survey.

was a virtual stagnation in literacy levels in the 1980s (see table 35 and figure 6). However, the current literacy rate of 84 per cent for Sri Lankan women is among the highest in the world and is nearly twice the average of 48 per cent estimated for low-income countries.

According to the data from the population censuses, the literacy rates for both males and females were higher in urban than in rural areas. In 1981, for instance, the literacy rate of rural females (79.9 per cent) was 11.1 percentage points lower than that of urban females. But according to the data from the sample surveys conducted in the 1980s and in 1990/91, while the literacy rates for urban and rural females were about the same in all three surveys, the rates for estate women were considerably lower; in 1990/91, the literacy rate for estate women (52.8 per cent) was 31.5 percentage points lower than that for rural and urban women (table 36).

Figure 6. Literacy rates of population aged 10 years and over by sex: 1901-1981

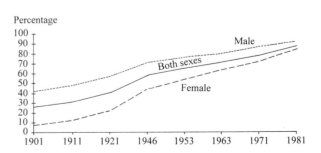

Source: Department of Census and Statistics.

Table 36. Literacy rates by sector and sex: 1971-1990/91

Source and year	Urban sector		Rural sector		Estate sector	
	Male	Female	Male	Female	Male	Female
1971 population census	90.3	81.5	84.1	67.9	–	–
1981 population census	95.3	91.0	89.0	79.9	–	–
1985/86 Labour Force and Socio-economic Survey	92.4	80.7	88.5	80.7	74.5	45.9
1986/87 Household Income and Expenditure Survey	96.2	86.5	94.1	86.5	82.9	56.3
1990/91 Household Income and Expenditure Survey[a]	94.0	84.3	89.9	84.3	79.0	52.8

Source: Department of Census and Statistics.

[a] Excluding Northern and Eastern provinces.

Age-specific literacy rates based on the 1985/86 and 1990/91 sample surveys indicate that gender differentials in literacy rates are minimal at ages below 40 years of age, or the population that had benefited from the expanded opportunities for education since the 1950s. At higher ages, the disparity increases with increasing age, reflecting historical trends in educational participation. According to the 1990/91 Household Income and Expenditure Survey, female literacy rates are slightly higher than the male rates at ages 10-24 years (table 37).

3. Health status

As noted earlier, Sri Lanka has made remarkable progress in enhancing the health status of its population, particularly that of women and children, during the past four decades owing to the adoption and implementation of pragmatic public health policies and programmes. Successive national governments had made genuine efforts to provide country-wide coverage of basic health services. Beginning in the 1940s, the country's health services were

Table 37. Age-specific literacy rates by sex: 1985/86 and 1990/91

Age group	1985/86			1990/91[a]		
	Both sexes	Male	Female	Both sexes	Male	Female
10-14	88.8	89.6	88.1	92.2	91.9	92.5
15-19	89.0	89.7	88.2	93.7	93.0	94.5
20-24	88.8	90.0	87.6	92.7	91.2	94.2
25-29	89.1	91.2	87.1	89.1	90.0	88.2
30-34	89.0	91.2	87.0	90.8	90.8	90.9
35-39	87.3	90.8	84.1	88.6	91.0	86.7
40-44	83.8	89.5	78.4	90.4	93.4	87.6
45-49	78.7	89.5	68.9	85.0	92.1	77.5
50-54	75.5	87.0	64.1	79.9	90.5	69.2
55-59	71.4	84.3	57.4	75.6	85.8	64.8
60-64	72.0	84.5	57.8	71.5	82.4	61.3
65 and over	61.8	75.8	48.2	61.1	77.8	44.3
All ages	84.2	88.6	80.0	86.9	90.0	83.8

Sources: (1) Labour Force and Socio-economic Survey, 1985/86
(2) Household Income and Expenditure Survey, 1990/91.

[a] Excluding Northern and Eastern provinces.

planned and implemented around the concept and principles of primary health care (PHC). A domiciliary service for mothers and special maternal and child health (MCH) services utilizing public health midwives, MCH clinics and institutional care at delivery are important features of the public health system, which has consistently accorded priority to mothers and children in view of their vulnerability.

Despite being a low-income country with a per capita GNP estimated at $US 570 in 1993, the health outcome indicators of Sri Lanka, such as crude death rate, infant mortality rate, maternal mortality rate and life expectancy at birth, are exceptionally good for a country at its level of per capita income, and compare favourably with those recorded for countries at much higher income levels. Nevertheless, Sri Lanka still experiences important health problems with persistent incidence of certain diseases, poor nutritional status of the population, and widespread disparity across districts in regard to morbidity patterns, reflecting to a large extent the influence of poverty and adverse physical environment among some segments of the population.

(a) Morbidity patterns and trends

Owing to the absence of relevant data disaggregated by gender, it is not possible to obtain a comprehensive picture of morbidity patterns and trends among females in the country. However, the available information indicates that the morbidity and ill-health rates are as high as in many other low-income countries, and that the pattern of disease is of a preventable nature owing to known causes. The most common diseases are diarrhoea, dysentery, acute respiratory infections, malaria, maternal and child undernutrition and anaemia.

Diarrhoeal diseases constitute the fifth leading cause of hospitalization, and rank as the third leading cause of death among infants in the country. While the number of cases admitted to government hospitals averages about 130,000-145,000 per annum, the number actually afflicted by diarrhoea is considerably higher, as only the severe cases are generally admitted

for in-patient treatment; others seek treatment from out-patient departments of government hospitals, private general practitioners, Ayurvedic physicians and others. A few limited studies suggest that children aged 0-4 years account for about 30 per cent of admissions for in-patient treatment in government medical institutions. Outbreaks of bacillary dysentery have been reported annually since August 1976, and it is now not only endemic in all parts of the country but is also the biggest problem among all diarrhoeal diseases in Sri Lanka.

Diseases of the respiratory system rank as the second leading cause of hospitalization in the country as a whole, and the first leading cause in eight districts. A 1987 survey of morbidity patterns and drug requirements at the primary health care level carried out in three health administrative regions, Anuradhapura, Kegalle and Ratnapura, revealed that approximately 25 per cent of the visits to out-patient departments were due to infectious and parasitic diseases, while another 18 per cent were due to diseases of the respiratory system.

Although malaria morbidity registered a significant decline during the period 1975-1985, available data suggest that its incidence has increased substantially since then in certain parts of the country, where it constitutes a major cause of morbidity. Further, there is considerable public resistance to domiciliary spraying of malathon in focal areas. Malaria is also a contributing cause of the high levels of anaemia among children and pregnant women.

A systematic assessment of the nutritional status of children and women in Sri Lanka is rendered difficult by the lack of comprehensive data at the national level. However, several limited surveys and small-scale studies indicate substantial undernutrition in young children and women by reference to international norms.

With regard to undernutrition in children, information on anthropometric measurements of height and weight of children in the age group 3-59 months collected in the 1987 and 1993 Demographic and Health Surveys suggests, by and large, a significant decline in the incidence of such undernutrition between 1987 and 1993. While there was a slight increase in the incidence of wasting (low weight-for-height, reflecting acute undernutrition), from 13 to 14 per cent, there have been significant declines in the incidence of stunting (low height-for-age, reflecting chronic undernutrition), from 27 to 21 per cent, and in the incidence of underweight (low-weight-for-height, reflecting both acute and chronic undernutrition) from 38 to 33 per cent. The incidence of stunting as well as of underweight was reported to be significantly higher among female children than among male children (table 38).

Low birthweight is an indicator of maternal nutrition, especially in the category of adequate nutrition in utero. According to the 1988/89 Nutritional Survey Status Reports prepared by the Ministry of Policy Planning and Implementation, about a fifth (19.6 per cent) of the babies are low-weight babies, this proportion being about 25 per cent among babies delivered at government hospitals in the Colombo area. Recent assessments at sentinel points by the Family Health Bureau reveal that the incidence of low birthweight babies is generally higher in rural areas (20.4 per cent) than in urban areas (15.0 per cent), and that in certain rural areas this incidence is as high as 30 per cent. The assessments also show that the incidence varied across the provinces, ranging from about 16 per cent in North-Central and Uva provinces to about 20 per cent in Southern Province (table 39).

Table 38. Incidence of moderate and severe malnutrition in children: 1987 and 1993

(Percentage)

Malnutrition indicator	1987			1993		
	Both sexes	Male	Female	Both sexes	Male	Female
Stunting	27	26	29	21	19	23
Wasting	13	12	13	14	14	14
Underweight	38	38	39	33	31	35

Source: W.R. Gunasekara, *Nutritional Status of Children in Sri Lanka* (Colombo, Department of Census and Statistics, July 1996).

Table 39. Percentage distribution of newborn babies by birthweight and by province and residence: 1988/89

Province/residence	Birthweight category			
	Normal	Low[a]	Unknown	Total
Province				
Western	72.5	17.2	10.3	100.0
Central	69.9	17.8	12.3	100.0
Southern	65.4	19.7	14.9	100.0
North Western	63.8	18.6	17.6	100.0
North Central	76.7	15.8	7.5	100.0
Uva	71.5	15.8	12.7	100.0
Sabaragamuwa	66.5	17.8	15.7	100.0
Residence				
Urban	72.5	15.0	12.5	100.0
Rural	66.5	20.4	13.1	100.0
Sri Lanka	69.7	17.5	12.8	100.0

Source: Family Health Bureau.

[a] Low birthweight = less than 2.5 kg.

The assessment of the Family Health Bureau is confirmed by the data from the 1993 Demographic and Health Survey, which also showed that the incidence of low birthweight is higher in rural and estate sectors than in the urban sector. According to the 1993 Survey, the incidence of low birthweight is significantly higher among female babies (21.0 per cent) than among male babies (16.7 per cent), among higher order births compared with second or third birth parities, and among children born to mothers with no education compared with those with secondary or higher educational attainments (table 40).

Table 40. Mean birthweight and incidence of low birthweight by background characteristics: 1993

Background characteristics	Mean birth-weight (kg)	Percentage low birth-weight (<2.5 kg)
Residence		
Colombo metro	2.9	19.4
Other urban	2.9	15.7
Rural	2.8	18.5
Estate	2.6	29.7
Education of mother		
No education	2.7	25.2
Primary	2.7	23.8
Secondary	2.8	17.7
More than secondary	2.9	15.6
Birth order		
First birth	2.8	19.4
2-3	2.9	16.8
4-5	2.8	21.8
6+	2.7	26.7
Sex of child		
Male	2.9	16.7
Female	2.8	21.0
Total	2.8	18.7

Source: Sri Lanka Demographic and Health Survey, 1993.

Several limited enquiries have shown a high prevalence of anaemia among pregnant women in the country. According to a 1973 survey, the prevalence of anaemia was about 62 per cent of the pregnant women covered in the study. A 1988/89 study conducted in respect of 692 pregnant mothers showed a prevalence rate of about 60 per cent, and of those, about 30 per cent were mildly anaemic, 28.3 per cent moderately anaemic and only 1.3 per cent severely anaemic. A 1990 sample study of women attending antenatal clinics showed that 65 per cent of the women included in the study were anaemic. The 1973 survey, referred to earlier, also showed a prevalence of anaemia among 68 per cent of non-pregnant women, 70 per cent of schoolchildren, and 38 per cent among men.

It is also important to note that a high prevalence of anaemia among pregnant women exists in spite of the distribution of iron and folate tablets at maternal and child health centres. The prevalence of anaemia is common among the lower socio-economic groups, and inadequate intake of iron, the chief cause of anaemia, has been revealed by several dietary surveys.

(b) Mortality patterns and trends

Since the latter part of the 1940s, Sri Lanka has experienced spectacular reductions in mortality rates owing to a combination of factors, such as an aggressive malaria eradication programme, expansion and improvements in health facilities, use of vaccine and antibiotics, spread of education, improved production and distribution of food, and other development programmes. Analytical studies also indicate that the substantial improvements in mortality conditions had benefited all segments of the population classified by age, sex, locality, ethnic groups etc. Indeed, as will be noted, women and children have benefited from these improvements more than have men and adults.

(i) Crude death rate

The crude death rates by sex for selected years from 1941 to 1989 are shown in table 41. It will be noted that, prior to 1960, the overall mortality rate for females was consistently higher than that for males, although the gap between the two rates was narrowing over the years. By 1960, the female rate was equal to the male rate, and since then the decline in the female rate has been faster than in the male rate, resulting in a widening difference in the mortality rates for females and males. In 1989, the female mortality rate of 4.5 per

Table 41. Crude death rate by sex: selected years, 1941-1989

Year	Male	Female	Female/male diference
1941	18.3	19.4	1.1
1946	19.6	22.1	2.5
1950	12.2	13.0	0.8
1956	9.6	10.1	0.5
1958	9.5	9.8	0.3
1960	8.6	8.6	–
1965	8.6	7.8	–0.8
1968	8.5	7.3	–1.2
1970	8.1	6.9	–1.2
1973	8.5	6.9	–1.6
1976	8.4	7.0	–1.4
1980	7.0	5.3	–1.7
1986	7.2	4.7	–2.5
1989	7.9	4.5	–3.4

Source: Registrar General's Department, Reports on Vital Statistics.

thousand was not only 3.4 points lower than the rate for males but also among the lowest in the world.

(ii) Age-specific death rate

As noted earlier in this section, until about the 1970s, female mortality rates were lower than male mortality rates at all ages excepting at the reproductive age group 15-44 years. However, during the past two decades, female rates have been lower than the corresponding male rates at all ages (table 42).

An examination of the cause-specific mortality rates for selected diseases in 1984 and 1989 indicates that during this period there was an increase in the rates for males as well as females in respect of diseases such as hypertension, ischaemic heart disease, chronic liver disease and cirrhosis and transport accidents. It will also be noted that in both years the rates for females were lower than the corresponding male rates for all diseases excepting anaemia. Although the incidence of mortality due to diseases of the respiratory system had declined during the five-year period, in 1989 these diseases were the most important cause of death among females, while suicides and self-inflicted injuries accounted for the largest number deaths among men (table 43).

(iii) Infant mortality rate

Over the years, Sri Lanka has made remarkable progress in reducing its infant mortality rates to reasonably low levels. At the beginning of this century, the infant mortality rate stood at about 177 per 1,000 live births, the rate for male infants (183.9) being significantly higher than that for female infants. Although these rates had declined to 156.0 for male and 141.6 for female infants by 1940, the 1940 rates were high in comparison with those obtaining in the more developed countries. Since 1940, there has been a dramatic decline in these rates, the male infant mortality rate falling by 43 per cent to 88.5 and the female

Table 42. Death rates by age group and sex: 1973, 1980 and 1989

Age group	1973		1980		1989	
	Male	Female	Male	Female	Male	Female
0-4	15.2	14.1	10.3	8.9	4.4	3.8
5-14	1.5	1.4	0.9	0.7	0.7	0.6
15-24	2.0	1.7	1.9	1.5	1.9	1.2
25-34	2.6	2.3	2.7	1.9	4.9	1.5
35-44	4.1	3.1	3.8	2.3	7.4	2.3
45-54	8.9	5.5	8.1	4.5	11.2	4.5
55-64	18.2	12.0	16.4	10.7	21.3	10.4
65-74	42.9	34.1	35.2	28.8	44.1	31.0
75+	150.9	140.1	131.3	123.3	114.8	103.7
All ages	8.5	6.9	7.0	5.3	7.9	4.5

Source: Registrar General's Department.

Table 43. Cause-specific mortality rates for selected diseases by sex: 1984 and 1989

Cause of death	1984		1989	
	Male	Female	Male	Female
Malignant neoplasm of respiratory and intra-thoracic organs	1.7	0.5	1.6	0.6
Anaemia	7.2	7.8	3.1	3.9
Hypertensive diseases	11.2	7.2	13.0	8.6
Mental disorders	2.1	0.9	3.9	1.0
Ischaemic heart diseases	27.2	9.1	35.5	15.3
Diseases of the upper respiratory tract	0.3	0.4	0.2	0.1
Other diseases of the respiratory system	47.1	37.7	35.9	25.9
Diseases of the gastro-intestinal tract	19.4	7.3	27.5	6.6
Chronic liver diseases and cirrhosis	6.3	1.2	15.1	1.8
Transport accidents	11.3	2.7	17.1	3.5
Accidental poisoning	3.1	1.2	2.5	0.6
Suicide and self-inflicted injuries	49.6	23.9	45.6	18.0

Source: Annual Health Bulletins, 1988 and 1993.

rate falling by 48 per cent to 74.3 per 1,000 live births in 1950. Thereafter, there were further declines, with the rate reduced to 21.7 per cent for male infants and to 18.5 per cent for female infants in 1988 (table 44). These rates are considerably lower than those estimated for many developing countries in the world. The fact that female infant mortality rates have been consistently lower than the male rates clearly indicates the absence of any discrimination against female children in regard to feeding and health care in Sri Lanka.

The remarkable improvement in infant mortality that has taken place particularly since the 1940s has been due to a number of factors, such as the provision of free health services; expansion and improvement of field and institutional services for mother and child; expanded programmes of immunization reaching universal coverage by the early 1990s; effective control of diarrhoeal diseases; provision of trained assistance at delivery and improved care at post-natal follow-up; and overall improvement in the quality of life of mothers.

The national average rates of infant mortality, however, mask significant disparities in these rates between various ethnic groups and administrative districts. Among the major ethnic groups, the Indian Tamils experience infant

Table 44. Infant mortality rate by sex: selected years, 1900-1988

Year	Both sexes	Male	Female	Male/female difference
1900	177.3	183.9	170.8	13.1
1910	176.0	183.4	168.5	14.9
1920	182.0	188.8	174.8	14.0
1930	174.7	183.8	165.7	18.1
1940	148.8	156.0	141.6	14.4
1950	81.4	88.5	74.3	14.2
1955	71.3	77.8	64.8	13.0
1960	56.8	61.6	51.9	9.7
1965	53.2	57.6	48.7	8.9
1970	47.5	51.5	43.3	8.2
1975	45.1	48.8	41.3	7.5
1978	37.2	40.2	34.1	6.1
1980	34.4	37.4	31.3	6.1
1983	28.4	30.4	26.3	4.1
1986	23.2	25.4	21.0	4.4
1988	20.2	21.7	18.5	3.2

Source: Department of Census and Statistics, *Changing Role of Women in Sri Lanka* (Colombo, 1997).

mortality rates which are more than twice the rate for the country as a whole. The rate for the "others" group, which mainly comprises the economically and socially backward community, was about 81 per 1,000 live births for female infants and 77 for male infants in 1988, nearly double the rate for Indian Tamils (table 45 and figure 7).

Table 45. Infant mortality rate by ethnic group and sex: 1976, 1982 and 1988

Ethnic group	1976		1982		1988	
	Male	Female	Male	Female	Male	Female
Sinhalese	40.0	35.5	32.5	25.9	20.4	17.2
Sri Lankan Tamil	35.3	30.8	26.4	20.7	19.7	17.3
Indian Tamil	117.2	101.0	72.4	58.5	49.6	44.3
Moor	42.2	35.9	25.2	25.9	17.3	14.0
Malay	31.8	19.4	29.4	9.7	3.8	17.3
Burgher	37.7	32.1	24.2	16.3	9.0	9.1
Others	88.8	67.0	27.1	19.0	76.9	81.1
All ethnic groups	46.6	40.7	33.8	27.1	21.7	18.6

Source: Registrar General's Department.

Figure 7. Infant mortality rate by ethnic group and sex: 1988

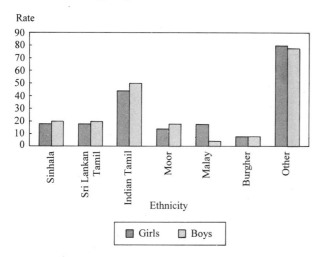

Source: **Department of Census and Statistics,** *Changing Role of Women in Sri Lanka* (Colombo, 1997).

There are also marked differences in infant mortality rates between the various administrative districts of the country. In 1988, the latest year for which official data are available, the female infant mortality rate was less than half the national average (18.5 per 1,000 live births) in Moneragala (7.1) and Hambantota (8.1) districts, while it varied between 10 and 13 per 1,000 live births in Kegalle (10.), Trincomalee (10.6), Polonnaruwa (11.6), Ampara (12.5), Matale (13.0) and Gampaha (13.4) districts. Nuwara Eliya stands out as the district with the highest female (32.3) as well as male (38.6) infant mortality rates in the country, while neighbouring Badulla (22.4), Kandy (25.8) and Ratnapura (23.9), together with Colombo (21.7), Matsava (22.1) and Anuradhapura (23.5), are districts

with a female infant mortality rate substantially higher than the national average. Although, in the past, the female infant mortality rate was lower than the male rate in all districts, in 1988 the female rate exceeded the male rate in Kilinochchi, Mannar, Vavuniya, Mullaitivu, Matara, Polonnavuwa and Moneragala districts (annex table C.7).

(iv) Child mortality rates

Child mortality, or deaths among children aged 1-4 years, exhibits a pattern which is altogether different from that of infant mortality. Available data for the 1980s indicate that while the mortality rate for both boys and girls aged 1-4 years has been declining over the years, the rate for girls has, by and large, been slightly higher than that for boys in the rural areas, and lower than that for boys in the urban areas. In 1988, however, the rate for girls and boys was equal in the rural areas. Further, child mortality rates for both sexes are substantially higher in urban than in rural areas (table 46).

(v) Maternal mortality rates

Along with the decline in general infant and child mortality rates, there was also a dramatic decline in maternal mortality rates, from about 1,500 per 100,000 live births in 1946 to 136 in 1971. As will be evident from table 47, the declining trend continued and in 1988, the maternal mortality rate of 38.6 per 100,000 live births was among the lowest in the world.

43

It is also clear from table 47 that, in general, maternal mortality declined in all age groups between 1971 and 1988, and in 1988 the risk of dying as a result of complications from pregnancy and childbirth was lowest for mothers aged 25-29 years and highest for those aged 45 years and over.

Apart from overall socio-economic development, the strengthening and expansion of the free field-based MCH programme of the Department of Health, improvement in institutional infrastructure, with trained female assistance at delivery and facilities to meet obstetric emer-gencies, have all contributed to the spectacular reduction in maternal mortality. The high level of literacy among women and their high rate of acceptance of family planning and birth-spacing practices have also contributed to the reduction in maternal mortality in Sri Lanka.

A large number of maternal deaths have been prevented by the high level of institutional care at delivery. According to the 1993 Demographic and Health Survey, 87.3 per cent of the births that occurred during the five years preceding the Survey took place at a government hospital or a maternity home, while

Table 46. Mortality rate for children aged 1-4 years by residence and sex: 1980-1988

Year	Sri Lanka		Urban		Rural	
	Boys	Girls	Boys	Girls	Boys	Girls
1980	2.8	2.9	7.1	7.3	2.0	2.1
1981	2.6	2.8	7.0	7.1	1.6	1.8
1982	3.4	3.3	10.2	8.8	1.9	2.1
1983	3.1	3.0	8.7	8.4	1.9	1.9
1984	3.1	3.1	8.3	8.1	1.9	2.0
1985	2.1	2.1	6.6	6.1	1.2	1.3
1986	1.8	1.8	5.6	5.1	1.0	1.1
1987	1.7	1.8	5.4	5.3	0.9	0.7
1988	1.3	1.3	4.5	4.2	0.7	0.7

Source: Department of Census and Statistics, *Changing Role of Women in Sri Lanka* (Colombo, 1997).

Table 47. Maternal mortality by age group: selected years, 1971-1988

(Per 100,000 live births)

Year	All ages[a]	15-19 years	20-24 years	25-29 years	30-34 years	35-39 years	40-44 years	45+ years	Maternal deaths as percentage of female deaths
1971	135.7	112.3	100.6	117.0	142.7	200.1	380.9	563.4	n.a.
1975	102.0	71.4	70.2	94.2	121.9	177.2	180.2	211.6	4.5
1980	64.5	50.4	48.3	52.2	56.1	169.8	125.4	258.0	3.9
1981	57.8	42.9	46.0	52.7	54.0	107.0	141.4	331.4	3.3
1982	60.2	52.2	50.2	48.3	54.3	120.9	124.0	676.2	3.6
1983	57.8	55.5	44.3	48.0	75.9	82.9	84.8	458.7	3.3
1984	44.0	40.7	35.7	36.8	46.4	66.3	109.8	550.7	2.4
1985	50.6	43.8	37.5	49.4	37.6	101.7	74.9	868.7	2.7
1986	47.0	62.5	37.3	37.3	51.2	68.3	82.1	543.5	2.5
1987	37.2	53.7	25.7	27.5	39.3	69.9	81.1	322.6	1.9
1988	38.6	35.0	33.3	28.1	34.9	77.5	101.1	728.2	1.9

Source: Registrar General's Department.

[a] Not including maternal deaths among mothers aged less than 15 years.

n.a. = not available.

another 6.5 per cent took place in a private nursing home. These proportions were higher in urban and rural areas than in estate areas (table 48).

The 1993 Survey also revealed that a very high proportion (94.1 per cent) of all births occurring during the five years preceding the Survey were assisted by a trained person, either a doctor or a nurse or a family health worker, while a further 4.6 per cent were assisted by traditional birth attendants. Nearly 99 per cent of the births in the urban areas and about 95 per cent of those in the rural areas took place under the supervision of trained personnel, but in the estate areas this proportion was about 70.0 per cent (table 49).

The national average maternal mortality rates, however, conceal the marked variation in this rate across the nine provinces. In 1988, the maternal mortality rate per 100,000 live births was lowest in Western Province (19.9), which is the most urbanized of the nine provinces, and lower than the national average (38.6) in Central and Southern provinces. But the rate was about double, or more than double, the national average in the war-torn Northern and Eastern provinces (table 50).

Available data (table 51) indicate that in 1980, hypertension was the leading cause of maternal mortality, accounting for over a third (35.6 per cent) of all maternal deaths, followed by haemorrhage (18.5 per cent) and abortion

Table 48. Percentage distribution of births in the five years preceding the 1993 Demographic and Health Survey, by place of delivery and residence

Residence	Place of delivery				
	Government hospital/ maternity home	Private nursing home	At home	Other	All places
Colombo metro	81.3	17.0	0.8	0.9	100.0
Other urban	66.6	32.2	1.2	–	100.0
Rural	91.6	2.8	5.4	0.2	100.0
Estate	70.0	0.3	29.8	–	100.0
Sri Lanka	87.3	6.5	6.0	0.2	100.0

Source: Department of Census and Statistics, *Sri Lanka Demographic and Health Survey, 1993* (Colombo, 1995).

Table 49. Percentage distribution of births in the five years prior to the 1993 Demographic and Health Survey, by type of assistance mother received during delivery and residence

Attendant assisting during delivery	Residence				
	Colombo metro	Other urban	Rural	Estate	Sri Lanka
Doctor	42.7	50.3	17.4	32.2	23.7
Government nurse/family health worker	56.3	49.1	77.2	38.1	70.4
Traditional birth attendant	0.2	0.6	3.4	16.6	3.6
Relative/neighbour	0.9	–	1.6	13.0	2.0
Other	–	–	0.2	0.1	0.2
No one	–	–	0.1	–	0.1
Total	100.0	100.0	100.0	100.0	100.0

Source: Department of Census and Statistics, *Sri Lanka Demographic and Health Survey, 1993* (Colombo, 1995).

Table 50. Maternal mortality by province: selected years, 1976-1988

(Rate per 100,000 live births)

Province	1976	1980	1985	1988
Western	34.3	41.4	24.4	19.9
Central	167.0	87.6	57.8	26.2
Southern	103.7	65.6	42.5	22.7
Northern	53.4	31.8	67.7	73.0
Eastern	99.8	91.0	55.8	79.6
North Western	107.0	71.8	72.2	47.9
North Central	97.2	65.9	69.3	47.1
Uva	104.2	95.2	56.0	48.6
Sabaragamuwa	77.4	59.1	50.9	39.6
Sri Lanka	93.2	64.5	50.6	38.6

Source: Registrar General's Department.

(10.7 per cent). However, during the next eight years, the relative importance of the leading causes changed, and in 1988 haemorrhage was the most important cause, accounting for 28.6 per cent of maternal deaths, while hypertension was the second most important (23.3 per cent). Abortion continues to account for over a tenth of all maternal deaths, reflecting the incidence of unwanted pregnancies and resort to unsafe or harmful methods of pregnancy termination.

Table 51. Percentage distribution of maternal deaths by major cause: 1980, 1985 and 1988

Major cause	1980	1985	1988
Abortion	10.7	11.2	10.5
Haemorrhage	18.5	31.5	28.6
Hypertension	35.6	23.9	23.3
Retained placenta	4.4	1.0	–
Major puerperal infections and sepsis	4.8	3.0	–
Other	25.9	29.4	37.6
Total	100.0	100.0	100.0

Source: Department of Census and Statistics, *Women and Men in Sri Lanka* (Colombo, May 1995).

(vi) Life expectancy

The tremendous success which Sri Lanka has achieved over the past five decades in re-ducing the incidence of morbidity and mortality is also reflected in the remarkable increase in the life expectancy of both males and females in the country. The expectation of life at birth, or average length of life, represents the average number of years that each member of a group of newborn infants could expect to live if throughout their lives they were to be exposed at each age to the risks of death reflected in the age-specific death rates of the period for which the life table is computed. The lower the level of mortality, the higher the longevity as measured by the life expectation at birth.

Two sets of estimates in regard to life expectancy by sex are available for Sri Lanka. The first set of estimates are those prepared from time to time by the Department of Census and Statistics, and may therefore be termed the "official estimates". The second set consist of estimates prepared by the Population Division of United Nations Headquarters as part of its periodic exercise of assessing changes in the size, growth and composition of the population of Member States of the United Nations, the latest assessment having been carried out in 1996. The official estimates and the United Nations estimates of life expectancy for both males and females are presented in table 52.

It is clear from the table that there is general agreement between the official and United Nations estimates in regard to life expectancy values at various points of time. Both sets of estimates show a steady increase in life expectancy at birth for both males and females, with greater gains for females than for males. Prior to the 1960s, the life expectancy for males was higher than that for females, but since the 1960s females have overtaken males in regard to longevity, with the gender gap increasing in favour of females over the years. As present, the average life expectancy of females in Sri Lanka is 4.5 years longer than their male counterparts. The country's current life expectancy rivals those of many middle-income countries and is very close to those of developed countries.

Table 52. Estimates of life expectancy at birth by sex

(Years)

Year	Official estimates[a]			Year	United Nations estimates[b]		
	Male	Female	Male/female		Male	Female	Male/female
1920-1922	32.7	30.7	2.0	1950/1955	57.6	55.5	2.1
1946	43.9	41.6	2.3	1955/1960	61.3	59.7	1.6
1953	58.8	57.5	1.3	1960/1965	63.3	63.7	−0.4
1962	61.9	61.4	0.5	1965/1970	63.5	65.9	−2.4
1965	63.7	65.0	−1.3	1970/1975	64.0	66.0	−2.0
1971	64.2	66.7	−2.5	1975/1980	65.0	68.5	−3.5
1981	67.7	72.1	−4.4	1980/1985	67.0	71.5	−4.5
1986	68.0	72.0	−4.0	1985/1990	68.5	73.0	−4.5
1991	69.5	74.2	−4.7	1990/1995	69.7	74.2	−4.5

[a] Department of Census and Statistics.

[b] United Nations, *World Population Prospects: The 1996 Revision* (forthcoming).

D. WOMEN IN FAMILY LIFE

1. The Sri Lankan family

In Sri Lanka, as in most countries in the world, the family or household has been and continues to be the basic unit of social life, performing numerous functions and providing various services to its members. Traditionally, the family/household has been the most common economic unit, involving a relatively efficient division of labour between husband, wife and children. In the agrarian setting, it has also served as the unit of economic production. The family/household has also served as the institution for childbearing and child-rearing and for providing emotional and physical support to its members. In turn, the family/household members have relied on and contributed to the numerous functions of the family in varying ways and degrees over the course of their lives.

While in the past the extended family, comprising not only parents and unwedded children but also married children, their spouses and offspring, had in most cases been the accepted pattern, today the nuclear family of father, mother and children constitutes the core of the family system and is also the most common type found among various ethnic groups in the country. In some instances, the nuclear family is extended by a close relative, usually an aged parent or a young unmarried sibling. Economic considerations and personal conve-

nience are the main reasons for the extension of the family in the rural areas. In those urban households where women have to work outside their homes, a female relative is invited to stay with the couple to take care of the children.

Data from the censuses and surveys indicate that in Sri Lanka the average family size has been shrinking, from 5.6 members in 1971 to 5.2 in 1981, according to the censuses conducted in those two years, and further to 5.0 in 1987 and to 4.7 in 1993, according to the Demographic and Health Surveys carried out in these two years. The 1993 Survey also revealed that the average family size varied from 4.3 in the estate or plantation sector to 4.9 in the rural sector and 5.4 in the urban sector. The decline in average family size has largely been attributed to the increasing tendency towards nuclearization of families and reduction in fertility rates.

In general, Sri Lankan families/households have traditionally been headed by men, generally the oldest male member in the family, who was perceived as the main economic provider of the family, with the other members being dependent on him. However, an analysis of the 1981 census data revealed the existence of a significant proportion (17.4 per cent) of households headed by women, and this proportion rose to 18.6 per cent, according to the

1994 Demographic Survey. In 1981, the proportion of female-headed households ranged from 10 to 20 per cent in Mannar, Mullaitivu, Moneragala and Anuradhapura districts, to 20 to 22 per cent in Matara, Galle and Jaffna districts. According to the 1994 Demographic Survey, which could not be carried out in the Northern and Eastern provinces, the proportion of households headed by women varied from a low of 13.2 per cent in Moneragala district to a high of 21.6 per cent in Matara district (table 53).

Table 53. Percentage of female-headed households by district: 1981 and 1994

District	1981	1994
Colombo	18.4	20.3
Gampaha	17.1	18.8
Kalutara	19.2	19.4
Kandy	18.6	20.7
Matale	15.5	18.9
Nuwara Eliya	15.9	15.7
Galle	22.3	21.0
Matara	22.0	21.6
Hambantota	19.3	18.5
Jaffna	20.4	–
Mannar	10.8	–
Vavuniya	12.7	–
Mullaitivu	11.0	–
Batticaloa	19.2	–
Ampara	15.7	–
Trincomalee	12.6	–
Kurunegala	16.5	18.7
Puttalam	17.3	17.8
Anuvadhapura	12.3	16.3
Polonnaruwa	12.8	15.7
Badulla	15.9	15.3
Moneragala	11.7	13.2
Ratnapura	14.7	15.2
Kegalle	17.2	19.7
Sri Lanka	17.4	18.6

Sources: 1981: Census of 1981.
1994: Demographic Survey.

Data from the 1981 census and the 1994 Demographic Survey also reveal that while the vast majority of male household heads (91.1 per cent in 1981 and 94.7 per cent in 1994) are married, the largest number of female household heads (48.0 per cent in 1981 and 55.8 per cent in 1994) are widowed. While the proportion of households headed by widows had increased between 1981 and 1994, there was a decline in the proportion of households

headed by married women, from 44.9 to 37.2 per cent during the same period. In 1994, the proportion of households headed by never-married on divorced/separated persons was significantly higher among female-headed then male-headed households (table 54).

Table 54. Percentage distribution of household heads by marital status and gender: 1981 and 1994

Marital status	1981		1994	
	Men	Women	Men	Women
Never married	6.0	5.0	2.6	4.5
Married	91.1	44.9	94.7	37.2
Widowed	2.5	48.0	2.3	55.8
Divorced/legally separated	0.4	2.0	0.4	2.5
All statuses	100.0	100.0	100.0	100.0

Sources: 1981: Census of 1981.
1994: Demographic Survey.

An analysis of the relevant data collected as part of the 1993 National Household Survey revealed that, for the country as a whole, the proportion of households headed by elderly persons aged 50 years and over was 70.8 per cent for female-headed households and 44.2 per cent for male-headed households; these proportions were about the same in urban as in rural areas (table 55).

The 1993 Survey also revealed that while the majority (66.0 per cent) of female-headed households had less than four family members, the majority of male-headed households (55.6 per cent) were large households with five or more members. The proportion of female-headed households having one to four members was considerably higher in the rural areas (68.7 per cent) than in the urban areas (53.7 per cent), while the proportion of male-headed households with five or more members was about the same in urban (56.3 per cent) as well as rural (55.2 per cent) areas (table 56).

The 1993 Survey also collected information regarding the difficulties perceived by female heads of households. While 31.6 per

Table 55. Percentage distribution of male and female household heads by age group and residence: 1993

Age group	Male head of household			Female head of household		
	Sri Lanka	Urban	Rural	Sri Lanka	Urban	Rural
15-29	5.8	5.9	5.8	2.1	1.3	2.3
30-39	20.8	22.5	20.4	9.5	13.4	8.7
40-49	29.1	26.1	29.8	17.5	13.7	18.3
50-59	20.6	21.0	20.5	20.6	22.3	20.3
60+	23.6	24.5	23.4	50.2	49.3	50.4
All ages 15+	100.0	100.0	100.0	100.0	100.0	100.0

Source: Department of Census and Statistics, *National Household Survey, 1993, Sri Lanka: Indicators on Selected World Summit Goals for Children and Women: Final Report* (Colombo, 1996).

Table 56. Percentage distribution of male and female household heads by household size and residence: 1993

Household size	Male head of household			Female head of household		
	Sri Lanka	Urban	Rural	Sri Lanka	Urban	Rural
1 member	2.4	1.3	2.6	10.2	6.1	11.1
2-4 members	42.2	42.4	42.2	55.8	47.6	57.6
5-6 members	39.3	36.1	40.1	24.7	27.7	24.0
7 and over members	16.1	20.2	15.1	9.3	18.6	7.2
All sizes	100.0	100.0	100.0	100.0	100.0	100.0

Source: Department of Census and Statistics, *National Household Survey, 1993, Sri Lanka: Indicators on Selected World Summit Goals for Children and Women: Final Report* (Colombo, 1996).

cent reported that they had no problems or difficulties, another 35.4 per cent reported that they experienced difficulties in getting work done and another 18.4 per cent reported loneliness as their main problem. Only 4.2 per cent of the female household heads considered lack of security to be their main problem (figure 8).

2. Family formation

(a) Marriage patterns

In Sri Lanka, as in most oriental countries, the marriage of daughters as well as of sons has traditionally been considered a sacred duty which should be performed as early as possible. In terms of the socio-cultural values of the indigenous ethnic groups, an unmarried or childless woman was regarded as an anomaly and was often debarred from taking part in weddings and other important social functions.

Figure 8. Difficulties perceived by female heads of households

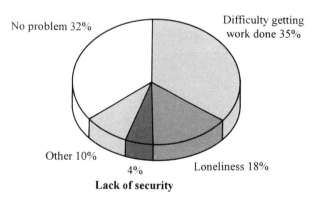

Source: National Household Survey, 1993, Sri Lanka.

Socio-cultural ethics also required that a man should marry and produce sons to ensure the continuity of the family lineage. Parents also deemed it to be their most important social duty to give their children in marriage once they attained marriageable age.

However, unlike in most oriental societies, child marriage was unheard of in Sri Lanka: a girl must attain puberty before she could be considered fit for marriage. The importance attached to the marriage of a girl is reflected in the elaborate ceremonies that are performed when she attains puberty. While in the past these ceremonies were regarded by all as of the utmost importance, today they are not rigidly observed, particularly among the well-educated sections of the population and among urban residents.

Monogamous marriages have generally been the rule among various ethnic groups in the country. Polygamy and polyandry, which were prevalent in certain areas of the Kandyan districts in the past, have now disappeared. Although polygamy was once practised among the Muslims, whose religion and laws permitted a man to have four wives at a time, this practice is now virtually non-existent among the Muslims.

Traditionally, marriages have been arranged by the family in accordance with certain rules of endogamy and exogamy. Among the Sinhalese and Tamils, marriages generally take place within the caste and religion. At the same time, there is social sanction against the marriage of parallel cousins. Among the Muslims, women are strictly forbidden to marry outside the religion. Dowry has also been an important consideration in most arranged marriages, though it does not appear to have been a prerequisite for marriage among low-income families. Since marriage is considered a fundamental social institution and is also expected to be irrevocable except for special reasons, marriage in Sri Lanka is always formalized, either through legal registration or through socially sanctioned customs.

In view of the sanctity attached to it, marriage has been nearly universal in Sri Lanka. According to the data from the 1946 census, for instance, the proportion of women ever-married was about 71 per cent at ages 20-24 years, increasing to nearly 95 per cent at ages 35-39 years. The corresponding proportions for men were considerably lower, but nearly 57 per cent at ages 25-29 years and 87.5 per cent at ages 35-39 years were reported to be ever-married in 1946.

Although marriage is still regarded as an important social institution in Sri Lanka, recent decades have witnessed very significant changes in marriage patterns in the country. Data from the censuses indicate that the proportion never-married among both men and women has been steadily increasing over the years, and that this increase has been more marked among women than among men, and among those at younger age groups compared with those at older ages. Between 1946 and 1981, the proportion of never-married women increased from 75.4 to 90.1 per cent at ages 15-19; from 29.4 to 55.3 per cent at ages 20-24; and from 11.8 to 30.4 per cent at ages 25-29 years. Even at ages beyond 30 years, there was an increase in the proportion of single women during this 35-year period (table 57).

Table 57. Percentage of never-married men and women at selected age groups: censuses of 1946 to 1981

Aged group	1946		1953		1963		1971		1981	
	Men	Women	Men	Women	Men	Women	Men	Women	Men	Women
15-19	98.8	75.4	98.7	75.7	99.0	85.0	99.4	89.4	99.0	90.1
20-24	80.5	29.4	83.5	32.5	84.7	41.3	86.6	53.2	83.4	55.3
25-29	43.4	11.8	45.4	12.8	50.2	17.1	53.2	24.6	51.4	30.4
30-34	22.4	6.6	21.7	7.5	26.1	8.3	25.6	10.9	24.9	15.8
35-39	12.5	4.3	11.8	5.4	13.1	4.8	13.4	5.8	12.6	8.9
40-44	9.3	4.1	8.7	5.0	10.3	4.3	9.2	4.7	8.3	5.9
45-49	7.6	3.4	7.6	4.6	7.4	3.9	8.0	4.1	6.9	4.4

Source: Department of Census and Statistics, reports of censuses of 1946, 1953, 1963, 1971 and 1981.

An increasing trend in the proportion of never-married men at various ages has also been reported by the four censuses from 1946 to 1971, but the pace of this increase has been slower than that for women because the corresponding proportions for men were already high in 1946 and considerably higher than those for women at each age group. Further, there was a slight decline in the age-specific proportions of never-married men between 1971 and 1981 (table 57).

As noted in the earlier sections of this profile, a census of the population has not been taken in Sri Lanka after 1981. However, the data from the two Demographic and Health Surveys conducted in 1987 and 1993 show that there were further increases in the proportion of never-married women at practically all ages from 15 to 49 years. According to the 1993 Survey, this proportion was 92.9 per cent at ages 15-19, 61.2 per cent at ages 20-24, and 33.7 per cent at ages 25-29 years (table 58).

Table 58. Percentage of never-married women at ages 15-49: 1987 and 1993

Age group	Percentage never-married women	
	1987	1993
15-19	92.7	92.9
20-24	57.3	61.2
25-29	30.0	33.7
30-34	14.2	17.7
35-39	9.1	11.1
40-44	6.2	9.2
45-49	3.5	5.2

Source: Department of Census and Statistics, *Sri Lanka Demographic and Health Survey,* 1987 and 1993, reported in *Women and Men in Sri Lanka* (Colombo, May 1995).

It is thus clear from tables 57 and 58 that during the 47 years between 1946 and 1993, the proportion of teenage girls (15-19 years) not entering wedlock increased by about one fifth, while that of women remaining single more than doubled at ages 20-24 years and almost trebled at ages 25-29 years. These trends would suggest that during the past few decades there has been a strong tendency among women, particularly those in the popular marriage ages 15-24, to delay their marriage and either enter into wedlock at a later age or remain single for life. It may also be noted that the fact that about 10 per cent of women at ages 40-44 and 5.2 per cent at ages 45-49 have been reported to be never married in 1993 means that marriage is no longer universal for Sri Lankan women.

It must, however, be emphasized that the change in nuptiality patterns occurring in Sri Lanka is not a new or peculiar phenomenon, because similar developments have been reported in respect of a large number of countries in the Asian and Pacific region. But what makes the Sri Lankan experience unique or outstanding is the scale at which these changes are taking place in the country. The proportion of never-married women at various ages is higher than in most other Asian countries, and in a South Asian context, this proportion in respect of women aged 15-19 is not only the highest in Sri Lanka but is also substantially higher than the corresponding proportions recorded for neighbouring countries. Indeed, the proportion of Sri Lankan girls remaining unmarried at ages 15-19 as well as the average age at first marriage for Sri Lankan women in 1981 approximate the respective values recorded for Ireland in 1988 (table 59).

The continuous increase in the proportion never married at various ages is also reflected in a rise in the singulate mean age at marriage in Sri Lanka. According to estimates based on census data the singulate mean age at marriage increased from 24.6 to 27.9 years for males and from 18.3 to 24.4 years for females between 1901 and 1981. The singulate mean age at marriage for women was reported by the Demographic and Health Surveys to be 24.8 years in 1987 and 25.5 years in 1993. The male/female difference in the singulate mean age at marriage also narrowed, from 6.3 years in 1901 to 3.5 years in 1981 (table 60).

The increase in the proportion of never-married women and the delay in marriage observed in recent decades are due to the combined effect of various socio-economic and demographic factors. As noted earlier, women's

Table 59. Percentage of never-married youth aged 15-19 years and average age at first marriage by sex for selected countries

Country	Year	Percentage never-married at ages 15-19 years		Average age at first marriage	
		Male	Female	Male	Female
Bangladesh	1981	93.3	31.2	23.9	16.7
India	1981	87.5	55.8	23.4	18.7
Maldives	1985	89.8	48.8	22.1	17.9
Nepal	1985	74.1	49.2	21.5	17.9
Pakistan	1981	92.5	68.9	24.9	19.8
Sri Lanka	1981	99.0	90.1	27.9	24.4
Ireland	1988	99.9	99.3	26.7	25.3

Source: W. Indralal De Silva, "Ireland of Asia: trends in marriage timing in Sri Lanka", *Asia-Pacific Population Journal,* vol. 12, No. 2, June 1997.

Table 60. Singulate mean age at marriage by sex: 1901-1993

Census/survey year	Singulate mean age at marriage		
	Male	Female	Difference
1901	24.6	18.3	6.3
1911	26.5	20.6	5.9
1921	27.0	21.4	5.6
1946	27.0	20.7	6.3
1953	27.2	20.9	6.3
1963	27.9	22.1	5.8
1971	28.0	23.5	4.5
1981	27.9	24.4	3.5
1987	–	24.8	–
1993	–	25.5	–

Source: Department of Census and Statistics, censuses of 1901 to 1981; and *Demographic and Health Survey,* 1987 and 1993.

participation in the education system, particularly at the secondary and tertiary levels, has increased tremendously over the years. This means that an increasing number of women aged 15-19 and 20-24 years, the hitherto popular marriage ages, are attending high schools or institutions of higher learning and are therefore currently not "available" for marriage. Further, the improved educational attainment of women has enabled most of them to obtain modern-sector employment with relatively high pay; and the ability to earn one's own living and the independence and security gained as a result have meant that marriage and childbearing may not be as central to a women's life now as they have been in the past. Higher levels of educa-

tion and employment have also increased the expectation of women in regard to the type of suitable partner.

An important demographic factor contributing to the observed increase in the proportion of unmarried women at various ages is the availability of male partners at appropriate marriage ages. In Sri Lanka, as in most other countries in the region, women tend to marry men who are about five years their senior in age. This would mean, for example, that women aged 15-19 years generally marry men aged 20-24 years, and women in the 20-24 age group marry men aged 25-29 years. In Sri Lanka, since women marry for the first time between ages 15 and 29 years and men between 20 and 34 years, the ratio of men aged 20-34 years to women aged 15-29 years should give a fairly reliable indication of the availability of men and women for marriage. These ratios for successive five-year age groups, based on the data from the censuses 1911 to 1981 and from the 1987 Demographic and Health Survey, are given in table 61.

It will be noted from table 61 that from 1911 to 1953 the ratio of males per 100 females in the appropriate "marriageable" age groups did not show any significant imbalances in the number of marriageable men and women as far as the popular ages (men aged 20-34 years and women aged 25-29 years) were concerned. Similarly, the male/female ratio for the ages at

**Table 61. Males per 100 females in selected age groups: censuses of 1911 to 1981
and Demographic and Health Survey, 1987**

Male/female ratio	1911	1921	1946	1953	1963	1971	1981	1987
Males (20-24 years)	114.8	111.1	103.7	116.4	87.7	95.3	96.9	95.3
Females (15-19 years)								
Males (25-29 years)	106.2	99.6	97.9	99.7	84.7	75.9	83.9	83.1
Females (20-24 years)								
Males (30-34 years)	87.2	86.4	91.2	84.5	95.4	79.5	89.4	82.6
Females (25-29 years)								
Males (20-34 years)	102.3	99.0	97.9	100.2	88.9	84.2	90.2	87.6
Females (15-29 years)								

Sources: Department of Census and Statistics, population censuses of 1911 to 1981, *and Sri Lanka Demographic and Health Survey, 1987.*

which practically all first marriages had then been taking place (20-24 years for men and 15-19 years for women) also did not show any sex imbalance during the period 1911-1953. However, since 1963, significant imbalances have been reported, with around 90 men in the age group 20-34 years for every 100 women in the 15-29 age group, except in 1971, when this ratio was 84.2. While the number of men aged 20-24 years per 100 women aged 15-19 years has shown a steady increase, from 87.6 in 1963 to 96.9 in 1981, at the next higher age level at which most first marriages had begun to take place, the ratio fluctuated between 1963 and 1981, and in 1981 there were only 84 men aged 25-29 years for every 100 women aged 20-24 years.

The relative availability of eligible men appears to have deteriorated further in the 1980s and, according to the 1987 Demographic and Health Survey, there were fewer than 88 men aged 20-34 years for every 100 women in the 15-29 age cohort. A deficiency of male partners has resulted in a "marriage squeeze", reducing considerably the chances of women to select their partners successfully.

Another important change in marriage practices that is reported to be taking place in Sri Lanka is the transition from arranged marriages to romantic or love marriages. In the past it was customary for parents or families to arrange marriages for their children, but in

recent decades marriages have increasingly tended to be the result of personal selection on the part of the two individuals concerned. This transition, however, is not a new phenomenon; available data indicate that even as far back as the early 1940s, about 25 per cent of the unions were love marriages. But the incidence of such marriages appears to have increased considerably over the years; according to the 1985 Contraceptive Prevalence Survey, love marriages constituted about 52 per cent of all marriages reported in that Survey.

The increase in the incidence of romantic or love marriages could be explained largely in terms of the expanding opportunities for female education and employment in the country. As noted earlier, an increasing proportion of women are engaged in secondary and higher-level education today as compared with about four decades ago and, as will be noted later in this profile, female employment outside the home has expanded rapidly over the years. Consequent upon these socio-economic developments, opportunities for meeting and falling in love are far greater for the current generation of young men and women than had been the case for the earlier generations. This trend is clearly attested to by the data collected in seven localities under the Sri Lanka Demographic Change Project in 1985, presented in table 62. A considerably higher proportion of women in the second generation with a high level of education have married romantically compared with previous generations.

Table 62. Percentage distribution of women by type of marriage, level of educational attainment and generation: 1985

Educational level	Generation and marriage type					
	Parent[a]		First generation[b]		Second generation[c]	
	Arranged	Love	Arranged	Love	Arranged	Love
Uneducated/less educated	71.9	28.1	58.2	41.8	28.7	71.3
Secondary	69.2	30.8	51.1	48.9	24.7	75.3
Higher than secondary	41.2	58.8	32.5	67.5	29.4	70.6
Total	47.1	52.9	37.5	62.5	25.3	74.7

Source: Sri Lanka Demographic Change Project, 1985, cited in Lakshman Dissanayake, "Factors influencing stabilization of women's age at marriage in Sri Lanka" (draft) (University of Adelaide, Australia, 1997).

[a] Last generation of parents with a high level of education.
[b] First generation with a high level of education.
[c] Second generation with a high level of education.

Various studies also reveal that the increasing trend towards romantic marriages is not peculiar to any one ethnic group or area but is taking place among all socio-cultural groups across the country. According to the data from the Sri Lanka Demographic Change Project, about 84 per cent of Sinhalese-Buddhist-Govigama caste women in the second generation with a high level of education married romantically, compared with 58 per cent of those in the first generation with a high level of education, while among a Muslim community living in a shanty area in Colombo, the proportion of women with a high level of education married romantically was about 43 per cent in the second generation compared with 27 per cent in the previous generation. An investigation carried out in a Muslim village in the south-central region of Sri Lanka in 1982 reported a high incidence of love marriages. The Project data also show that the incidence of love marriages is higher in urban than in rural areas.

(b) Reproductive behaviour

Concurrent with the shift in marriage patterns and practices, Sri Lanka has also experienced remarkable changes in the reproductive behaviour of women during the past few decades. In particular, the attitude of Sri Lankan women towards family size has undergone a very significant transformation. These changes are reflected in the trends in various indicators over time.

Data from the vital registration system as well as from various sample surveys show conclusively a marked reduction in TFR, or the average number of births a woman would have during her reproductive period if she survived throughout that period and experienced the same age-specific fertility rates as those prevailing during the period of reference. It must, however, be emphasized that a comparison of the results from various sources should be undertaken cantiously, for various reasons. In the first instance, while data prior to 1981 are representative of the entire country, those from the Demographic and Health Surveys of 1987 and 1993 do not cover the Northern and Eastern provinces owing to the civil war. Second, measures based on the two Surveys are calculated for a period of years preceding the Surveys, while those for earlier years refer to single calendar years.

It is clear from table 63 that there was a continuous decline in TFR from 5.0 in 1963 to 2.3 in 1988-1993, except for an increase in 1981 brought about by a temporary increase in fertility among women aged 15-34 years. In other words, today an average Sri Lankan woman would give birth to a total of 2.3 children compared with her counterpart about

Table 63. Age-specific fertility rates and total fertility rate: 1963 to 1988-1993

Age group	1963 Vital statistics	1974 WFS 1975	1981 CPS 1982	1982-1987 DHS 1987	1988-1993 DHS 1993
15-19	0.052	0.031	0.034	0.038	0.035
20-24	0.228	0.146	0.172	0.147	0.110
25-29	0.278	0.161	0.222	0.161	0.134
30-34	0.240	0.158	0.177	0.122	0.104
35-39	0.157	0.126	0.099	0.071	0.054
40-44	0.046	0.043	0.037	0.023	0.014
45-49	0.007	0.006	–	0.003	0.004
TFR	5.0	3.4	3.7	2.8	2.3

Source: Department of Census and Statistics, *Sri Lanka Demographic and Health Survey, 1993* (Colombo, February 1995).

Note: WFS = World Fertility Survey.
CPS = Contraceptive Prevalence Survey.
DHS = Demographic and Health Survey.

30 years ago. The spectacular decline in fertility has also occurred among Sri Lankan women in various reproductive age groups.

The decline in fertility is also confirmed by data on completed fertility or number of children ever born to ever-married or currently married women aged 45-49 years. Data from various surveys indicate that the mean number of children ever born declined from 6.0 in 1975 to 4.0 in 1993 for ever-married women, and from 6.3 in 1975 to 4.0 in 1993 for currently married women aged 45-49 years. It will be noted that there is hardly any difference in these figures related to both categories of women who have completed their reproductive cycle. It is, however, important to note that during a period of less than 20 years there has been a decline in the mean number of children ever born by one third in the case of ever-married women and by about 37 per cent in respect of currently married women, and that between 1987 and 1993 there was a decline of about 22 per cent (table 64).

The reduction in TFR by more than 50 per cent over a 30-year period has been brought about by two important factors: increase in female age at marriage and decline in marital fertility or fertility within marriage. Various studies have shown that the rise in age at marriage was responsible for more than half (52.6 per cent) of the decline in fertility between 1963 and 1981, although it accoun-

Table 64. Mean number of children ever born for women aged 45-49 years: 1975-1993

Year and data source	Mean number of children ever born	
	Ever-married women aged 45-49 years	Currently married women aged 45-49 years
1975 World Fertility Survey	6.0	6.3
1982 Contraceptive Prevalence Survey	5.8	5.8
1987 Demographic and Health Survey	5.1	5.1
1993 Demographic and Health Survey	4.0	4.0

Source: Department of Census and Statistics, *Sri Lanka Demographic and Health Survey, 1993* (Colombo, February 1995).

ted for only about one fifth (27.6 per cent) of the decline between 1971 and 1981. Since the mid-1970s, the decline in marital fertility owing to increase in contraceptive practice has been responsible for the further decline in fertility in Sri Lanka.

Data from various surveys indicate that there has been a remarkable increase in knowledge about and use of contraception among all segments of the population. According to data from the two Demographic and Health Surveys of 1987 and 1993, knowledge about contraception is almost universal, with around 99 per cent of ever-married as well as currently married women reporting knowledge of at least one method of contraception, and virtually all of them also know a modern method. Between 1987 and 1993, the proportion of women reporting knowledge about traditional methods increased by about four percentage points, from 67 to 71 per cent for ever-married women and from 68.3 to 72.6 per cent for currently married women (table 65).

The 1993 Demographic and Health Survey also revealed that knowledge about all modern methods was uniformly high (more than 98 per cent) among women in all age groups except the youngest (15-19 years), in respect of whom it was slightly lower (96.3 per cent). But the proportion of women reporting knowledge of traditional methods was considerably lower among the youngest age group (47.1 per cent) compared with 72.6 per cent for all women aged 15-49 years (table 66).

Data from various surveys indicate that the proportion of ever-married women who have ever used a contraceptive method has increased steadily, from 46.5 per cent in 1975 to 76.2 per cent in 1993, and that the proportion

Table 66. Percentage of currently married women aged 15-49 years knowing any method, any modern method and any traditional method of contraception, by current age of women: 1993

Current age of women	Percentage with knowledge of		
	Any method	Any modern method	Any traditional method
15-19	96.3	96.3	47.1
20-24	98.9	98.9	66.2
25-29	99.7	99.7	69.4
30-34	99.1	99.1	76.3
35-39	99.7	99.7	76.9
40-44	99.8	99.8	75.6
45-49	98.5	98.4	70.7
Total	99.3	99.3	72.6

Source: Department of Census and Statistics, *Sri Lanka Demographic and Health Survey,* 1993 (Colombo, February 1995).

ever using a modern method more than doubled, from 27.4 to 56.9 per cent, during this period (table 67).

According to evidence from the various surveys, the proportion of currently married women aged 15-49 years currently using a method

Table 65. Percentage of ever-married and currently married women aged 15-49 knowing any method, any modern method and any traditional method of contraception: Demographic and Health Surveys of 1987 and 1993

Contraceptive method	Ever-married women		Currently married women	
	1987	1993	1987	1993
Any method	**98.8**	**99.1**	**99.1**	**99.3**
Any modern method	**98.7**	**99.0**	**99.1**	**99.3**
Pill	92.7	93.8	93.4	94.5
IUD	82.4	84.9	83.4	85.7
Injection	83.3	91.3	84.3	92.0
Vaginal methods[a]	14.3	11.2	14.6	11.6
Condom	72.2	77.6	73.3	78.7
Female sterilization	97.7	97.0	98.1	97.3
Male sterilization	90.8	88.2	91.5	88.6
Norplant	5.5	10.0	5.8	10.5
Any traditional method	**67.0**	**71.0**	**68.3**	**72.6**
Periodic abstinence	60.7	64.3	61.9	65.9
Withdrawal	37.8	49.7	38.8	51.3
Other	1.4	2.1	1.4	2.1

Source: Department of Census and Statistics, *Sri Lanka Demographic and Health Survey,* 1993 (Colombo, February 1995).

[a] Vaginal methods are diaphragm, foam and jelly.

Table 67. Percentage of ever-married women who have ever used a contraceptive method, by major method: 1975-1993

Year and data source	Any method	Any modern method	Any traditional method
1975 World Fertility Survey	46.5	27.4	30.0
1982 Contraceptive Prevalence Survey	69.2	41.0	46.6
1987 Demographic and Health Survey	71.8	50.4	44.3
1993 Demographic and Health Survey	76.2	56.9	43.5

Source: Department of Census and Statistics, *Sri Lanka Demographic and Health Survey, 1993* (Colombo, February 1995).

Note: Data from the Northern and Eastern provinces have been excluded from the 1975 and 1982 Surveys to render their findings comparable with those of the 1987 and 1993 Surveys.

of contraception almost doubled, from 34.4 per cent in 1975 to 66.1 per cent in 1993. As well, the proportion currently using a modern method (43.7 per cent) was almost double that of those using a traditional method (22.4 per cent). The major change in the method mix has been an increase in sterilization use from about 11 per cent in 1975 to about 30 per cent in 1987, and thereafter a slight decline to 27.2 per cent in 1993. The use of all other modern temporary methods, such as pills, IUD, injectibles and condoms, had remained more or less constant, at around 10 per cent, until 1987, thereafter increasing to 16.5 per cent in 1993. Traditional method use, which has always been relatively high in Sri Lanka compared with other countries, increased from 14.2 per cent in 1975 to 26.0 per cent in 1982, and was reported to be 22.4 per cent in 1993 (table 68).

The national averages relating to proportions using contraceptives mask the wide variations in these proportions between sectors, zones

Table 68. Trends in current contraceptive use by method among currently married women aged 15-49 years: 1975-1993

Contraceptive method	1975 World Fertility Survey	1982 Demographic and Health Survey	1987 Demographic and Health Survey	1993 Demographic and Health Survey
Pill	1.7	2.7	4.1	5.5
IUD	5.2	2.9	2.1	3.0
Injection	0.4	1.0	2.7	4.6
Condom	2.3	3.3	1.9	3.3
Sterilization	10.6	22.0	29.8	27.2
Norplant	–	–	–	0.1
Periodic abstinence	8.9	14.2	14.9	15.2
Withdrawal	1.6	5.1	3.4	5.0
Other	3.7	6.7	2.8	2.2
Any modern method	**20.2**	**31.9**	**40.6**	**43.7**
Modern temporary	9.6	9.9	10.8	16.5
Sterilization	10.6	22.0	29.8	27.2
Any traditional method	**14.2**	**26.0**	**21.1**	**22.4**
Any method	**34.4**	**57.9**	**61.7**	**66.1**

Source: Department of Census and Statistics, *Sri Lanka Demographic and Health Survey, 1993* (Colombo, February 1995).

Note: Data from the Northern and Eastern provinces have been excluded from the 1975 and 1982 Surveys to render their findings comparable with those of the 1987 and 1993 Surveys.

and women with different levels of educational attainment. It is evident from annex table D.1 that the proportion of currently married women aged 15-49 years not currently using any contraceptive method is lowest (31.7 per cent) in rural areas and highest (45.5 per cent) in the estate areas. Surprisingly, this proportion is also fairly high (42.3 per cent) in "other" urban areas. It is also interesting to note that the use of sterilization is highest (44.4 per cent) and the use of traditional methods lowest (7.0 per cent) among estate women.

Among the seven zones, the proportion not currently using any method is highest (37.3 per cent) in zone 1, which comprises the Colombo metropolitan area, consisting of some urban areas in Colombo and Gampaha districts, followed by zone 5, which covers the South-Central hill country with a concentration of estates, and is lowest (28.9 per cent) in zone 2, which encompasses the Colombo feeder areas. The proportion resorting to sterilization is highest in zone 5 (36.9 per cent), closely followed by zone 6, which includes the irrigated dry zone with major and minor irrigation schemes.

In terms of educational background, non-use of contraception is highest (41.8 per cent) among women with no education. The proportion using traditional methods increases with the rise in the level of educational attainment, this proportion among women with more than secondary education (29.2 per cent) being almost three times that among women with no education (10.4 per cent).

3. Marital disruption

Persons who are widowed or divorced/separated are considered to be living in a state of marital disruption. Data from the 1981 censuses indicate that the overall incidence of widowhood as well as divorce and legal separation is relatively low in Sri Lanka, with about 5 per cent of all women aged 15 years and over being reported as widowed and less than 0.5 per cent as divorced or legally separated. Further, compared with elderly women aged 50 years and over, the incidence of widowhood is very much less among women in the reproductive ages 15-49, and less than one per cent among women between 15 and 30 years of age (table 69).

Table 69. Age-specific proportions of widowed and divorced/separated persons by sex: 1981 census

Aged group	Widowed		Divorced/ separated	
	Male	Female	Male	Female
15-19	–	0.1	–	0.1
20-24	0.1	0.5	0.2	0.5
25-29	0.2	1.0	0.3	0.7
30-34	0.3	2.0	0.5	0.9
35-39	0.6	3.9	0.6	1.0
40-44	1.0	7.0	0.7	1.0
45-49	1.8	11.1	0.8	0.9
50-54	2.9	11.4	0.7	0.8
55-59	4.2	22.8	0.7	0.7
60-64	6.5	31.4	0.7	0.6
65+	13.3	47.7	0.6	0.4
All ages	1.2	5.2	0.3	0.4

Source: Department of Census and Statistics, census of 1981.

Marriage data from the Registrar General's Department indicate that, although about 98 per cent of all marriages in the country take place between bachelors and spinsters, in recent years there has been an increase in the remarriage of widows and divorced women to bachelors, widowers or divorced men (table 70). This would suggest that any incidence of marital disruption through widowhood or divorce is to a large extent compensated by remarriage.

4. Domestic violence

The increasing incidence of violence against women, which has been a matter of great concern for some years, has now assumed the proportions of an important national social problem. Several studies in this area have identified the different types of violence against women commonly prevalent in Sri Lanka: domestic violence, incest, homicides in the family, sexual assault, rape, and sexual harassment at the workplace. However, it is not possible to draw a strict division between these various types of violence against women, since there is an overlap among most of them.

Table 70. Marriages by type and civil condition: 1983, 1985 and 1988

Civil condition	1983		1985		1988	
	Number	Percent-age	Number	Percent-age	Number	Percent-age
Bachelors who married						
Spinsters	120 688	97.5	125 677	97.5	129 421	97.7
Widows	614	0.5	467	0.4	494	0.4
Divorced women	337	0.3	393	0.3	431	0.3
Widowers who married						
Spinsters	938	0.8	845	0.7	750	0.6
Widows	305	0.2	436	0.3	213	0.2
Divorced women	77	0.1	65	0.1	85	0.1
Divorced men who married						
Spinsters	615	0.5	717	0.6	803	0.6
Widows	34	–	63	–	46	–
Divorced women	122	0.1	195	0.2	276	0.2
Total	123 731	100.0	128 858	100.0	132 520	100.0

Source: Registrar General's Department.

It is a great tragedy that, for most abused women, violence begins at home, with the husbands, fathers, brothers or other male relatives being the main perpetrators. Domestic violence against women and female children is a form of gender-based violence which has no ethnic, religious, class or caste bias. As in most other countries of the region, a very high proportion of such violent acts remain unreported and are thus "a hidden issue" because the victims are generally reluctant to file complaints with law enforcement authorities.

The main reason why women are reluctant to report abuse in the home is their unequal status within the family as well as in society, and there are no viable alternatives available to them except to become resigned to living in an abusive domestic environment. Economic dependence, fear for their lives, shame, social pressures, lack of confidence, fear of initiating any action that may result in the husband or other male family member losing their jobs, as well as the attitude of the police, prevent women from reporting domestic violence. In fact, a survey conducted by the Centre for Women's Research revealed that most women accepted or conceded the right of their husbands to beat them, particularly in a domestic controversy, and such violent conduct

on the part of the husband was justified as it was brought about due to their "own fault".

For various reasons stated above, the data from the Crimes Division of the Police Department do not indicate the true magnitude of domestic violence against women and children in the country. It is also well known that even when such incidents are reported, the law-enforcement authorities tend to treat such complaints as purely "domestic affairs". Despite these lapses, available data indicate that the number of reported cases of domestic violence against women increased by 27 per cent from 40,979 in 1990 to 52,168 in 1991, and that nearly two thirds of these complaints related to harassment, insult and intimidation by husbands, while nearly a third related to assault by husbands (table 71).

Another area of concern is the increasing incidence of incest. The actual situation is much worse than is perceived by the society, as underreporting of incest is more the rule than the exception. A very high degree of social stigma is attached to incest and a greater degree of coercion exerted by assailants to prevent victims from reporting. Unlike in rape cases, there is also a higher probability of incest being totally covered up.

Table 71. Numerical and percentage distribution of reported cases of domestic violence against women by broad category of offence: 1990 and 1991

Type of offence	1990		1991	
	Number	Percentage	Number	Percentage
Assault by husbands	13 368	32.6	19 656	37.7
Harassment, insult and intimidation	27 611	67.4	32 512	62.3
Total	40 979	100.0	52 168	100.0

Source: I.T. Canagaretnam, "Role of the enforcement authorities in the prevention of violence against women", paper presented at the Workshop on Violence Against Women (Colombo, Women's Bureau, 1992).

E. WOMEN IN ECONOMIC LIFE

1. Background

In Sri Lanka, women have traditionally played an important role in economic production, thereby contributing significantly to their family/household incomes as well as to GNP. In the rural agricultural sector, women have participated in paddy cultivation, although there was a distinct division of labour between males and females. In general, men assumed responsibility for the more strenuous type of chores such as ploughing, hoeing and preparing the land for cultivation, while women were entrusted with weeding, transplanting, harvesting and food processing and preparation. Women have also assisted the men in slash-and-burn cultivation, and had major responsibility for home gardening and livestock- and poultry-raising. Besides farming and animal husbandry, women have engaged in other income-generating activities, mostly home-based cottage industries. The participation of women in various economic activities was in addition to their performing arduous domestic chores such as cleaning and maintenance of the house, fetching water and fuel for domestic use, the preparation of meals for family members, and taking care of the young children.

Despite the fact that women have devoted a substantial portion of their time and energy to economically productive activities, particularly in the subsistence sector, their contributions to production have not been taken into account adequately either in the labour-force data or in the national income statistics. As in most other developing countries, there has been a tendency in Sri Lanka to treat women's participation in family farm work and home-based income-generating activities as unpaid family work. Indeed, most women engaged in such activities have reported themselves as housewives, and have therefore been enumerated either as unpaid family workers or as being not economically active in past censuses and labour-force surveys. Consequently, according to the data from these sources, the labour-force participation rates for females were considerably lower than those for males.

It must, however, be noted that data from censuses and surveys reflect almost fully the participation of women in the commercial plantation or estate sector where they are employed as paid labourers. Women constitute half the plantation workers and are the largest group of organized women workers in Sri Lanka. Further, with extended educational facilities and rising levels of educational attainment, an increasing number of females have in recent years found employment in the modern formal sector, in which employment opportunities have been expanding since the late 1970s owing to a sharp shift in economic strategies from the inward-oriented regulated economy of earlier years to a liberal, open economic policy aimed at creating conditions for sustained economic growth. Women with lesser educational attainments have also been absorbed into the formal labour market, particularly in the garment and other industries which require low levels of skills, as well as in the informal sector. Women workers in the informal sector are usually not included in official labour market statistics, nor are they referred to in official policy and plan documents.

Despite the growth in female employment opportunities, available data and information clearly indicate that women workers are generally concentrated in low-status, low-skill, and low-paid jobs in subsistence and plantation agriculture, in small industries and modern assembly line industries and in petty trade in the informal sector, Further, labour-force data reveal that female unemployment rates are almost double the rates for males, and that among secondary school-leavers females experience greater difficulty than males in finding employment. A major reason for the disadvantageous situation in which women find themselves in the economic sphere is the general perception among planners and policy makers that women are essentially dependent housewives or, at best, secondary earners who merely help to augment family incomes through their activities. It is seldom recognized that among low-income groups, females are often primary income-earners responsible for the survival and maintenance of their families, and that the poorer the family, the greater is the need for the earnings of the female members.

2. Data sources and limitations

Population censuses, labour-force enquiries and other sample surveys have traditionally been the major sources of data and information on the economic activity of the population aged 10 years and over in Sri Lanka. Although the censuses since 1946 have adopted the "gainful worker" concept instead of the "earner" concept adopted in the earlier censuses to enumerate the economically active population, the definition of "gainful worker" had varied from one census to another. For example, the 1946 and 1953 censuses enumerated the unemployed persons with previous experience as part of the gainfully employed. But in 1963, all those without employment, whether previously employed or not, were considered unemployed and their particulars recorded only if they were actively seeking employment. At the 1971 census, all those without employment were considered unemployed if they were available for work, irrespective of whether they were actively seeking employment or not.

Similarly, the unpaid family workers were excluded from the category of gainful workers but were included in this category in the subsequent censuses. Consequently, the time series

data on economic activity provided by the censuses are subject to limitations imposed by changes in the definitions and concepts adopted. However, in view of the more or less close agreement between these concepts since the 1963 census, an analysis of economic activity in this section will be based on the data from censuses carried out in 1963 and thereafter. Further, since the 1990 round of censuses was not carried out in the country owing to the civil war in the northern and eastern parts of the island, the analysis of labour-force participation will be based on the data from the labour-force surveys conducted in 1985/86, 1992, 1995 and 1996. These surveys were not conducted in the war-torn Northern and Eastern provinces.

3. Labour-force participation

The total population aged 10 years and over, as well as the economically active population (or labour force), by activity, status and gender, as reported at the censuses of 1963, 1971 and 1981, and the Sri Lanka Labour Force Surveys conducted in 1985/86, 1992, 1995 (First Quarter) and 1996 (First Quarter) are shown in annex table E.1. It will be noted from this table that while up to 1981 males outnumbered females among the population of working ages (10 years and over), the Labour Force Survey data from 1985/86 onwards indicate a slight excess of females over males among persons of working age, except in 1992, when the number of males and females was almost equal. In 1996, there were 102.2 females per 100 males at ages 10 years and over in the country.

It will also be noted from annex table E.1 that the number of persons reported as economically active or in the labour force increased considerably among both males and females in the country between 1963 and 1996, but that this increase was more marked among females than among males. Whereas the male labour force increased by about 150 per cent, from 2,713,779 in 1963 to 4,125,645 in 1996, the female labour force more than trebled, from 708,542 to 2,171,523, during the same 33-year period.

The overall labour-force participation rates, or persons in the labour force as a proportion of the population aged 10 years and over, derived from the data in annex table E.1 are given in table 72. It is clear from the table that while the overall participation rate for males declined, with some fluctuations, from 69.3 per cent in 1963 to 65.3 per cent in 1996, that for females increased almost steadily, from 20.0 to 33.5 per cent during the same period. Nevertheless, even in 1996, the overall female participation rate was about 32 percentage points less than or nearly half the corresponding rate for males.

The age-specific labour-force participation rates based on the data from the 1971 and 1981 censuses as well as from the 1985/86, 1992 and 1995 Labour Force Surveys are given in table 73. It is evident from this table that the rates for females have always been lower than those for males at all age groups, and that,

Table 72. Overall labour-force participation rates of persons aged 10 years and over by sex: censuses of 1963 to 1981 and Labour Force Surveys of 1885/86, 1992, 1995 and 1996

Year and data source	Overall labour-force participation rate (percentage)		
	Both sexes	Male	Female
1963 census	45.9	69.3	20.0
1971 census	48.0	68.5	26.0
1981 census	44.3	64.9	22.9
1985/86 Labour Force Survey	50.3	68.6	32.6
1992 Labour Force Survey[a]	47.7	64.3	31.1
1995 Labour Force Survey[a]	47.8	63.8	32.1
1996 Labour Force Survey[a]	49.1	65.3	33.5

Sources: Department of Census and Statistics, reports of the censuses of population and housing of 1963, 1971 and 1981; and reports of the Sri Lanka Labour Force Surveys of 1985/86, 1992, 1995 and 1996.

[a] Excluding Northern and Eastern provinces.

Table 73. Labour-force participation rates by age group and sex: 1971-1995

(Percentage)

Age group	1971 census		1981 census		1985/86 Labour Force Survey		1992 Labour Force Survey[a]		1995 Labour Force Survey[a] (First Quarter)	
	Male	Female	Male	Female	Male	Female	Male	Female	Male	Female
10-14	6.0	4.0	5.5	2.4	6.8	4.2	1.9	1.3	1.0	0.5
15-19	48.3	26.7	40.4	19.0	45.5	24.2	32.0	21.1	32.9	22.1
20-24	88.9	43.1	78.7	36.8	87.4	48.3	85.5	54.5	82.5	57.3
25-29	96.9	40.2	89.9	36.5	96.6	46.2	94.0	49.9	94.5	56.5
30-34	97.7	35.2	93.4	33.7	96.2	44.9	96.3	44.4	98.4	45.5
35-39	97.5	32.9	94.1	32.1	97.9	45.1	97.1	46.7	95.7	48.9
40-44	96.8	30.8	93.1	28.7	96.3	45.0	96.2	43.4	95.0	46.0
45-49	95.7	29.5	91.7	25.6	95.8	42.2	93.5	38.0	92.2	42.3
50-54	92.3	24.7	86.9	19.8	91.5	38.0	85.8	27.6	89.8	20.1
55-59	81.1	17.6	73.4	13.3	84.6	26.1	73.4	23.6	70.6	26.1
60 and over	50.6	7.3	43.5	5.3	52.2	14.2	41.0	8.4	32.1	6.3
All ages 10+	68.5	26.0	64.8	23.1	68.6	32.5	64.3	31.1	63.8	32.1

Sources: Department of Census and Statistics, reports of the censuses of population and housing of 1971 and 1981; and reports of the Sri Lanka Labour Force Surveys of 1992 (Final Report) and Sri Lanka Labour Force Survey, 1995 (First Quarter).

[a] Excluding Northern and Eastern provinces.

by and large, the gender disparity in participation rate rises with increasing age after age 40. At ages 50 years and over, the male rates are more than double the female rates.

It will also be noted from table 73 that in terms of the data from the Labour Force Surveys, there was a decline between 1985 and 1995 in the participation rates of both males and females at ages 10-14 and 15-19, reflecting to a large extent the increasing participation of boys and girls in the education system. However, the trend in the age-specific participation rates for females is different from that of males at ages 20-44 years. The female participation rates at these ages indicated an increasing trend between 1981 and 1995, owing largely to the rising educational levels of women and expanding opportunities for female employment. In the case of males, there was a fluctuation in the participation rates at all age groups between 20 and 44 years, the general pattern being one of stabilization of these rates at fairly high levels.

It is also evident from table 73 that the participation rate rises steeply with age up to age 20-24 years for both males and females, but thereafter the trend is different for males and females. The male rates continue to rise to reach a peak at the mid-20s and remain almost constant at a high level until the late 40s, thereafter declining, first gradually and then more steeply. In the case of females, the peak participation is reached at ages 20-24

years, and thereafter the rate declines gradually until the late 40s, and more sharply at older ages (see also figure 9).

Figure 9. Labour-force participation rate by age and sex: 1992

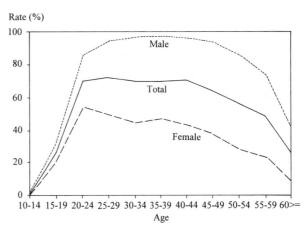

Source: Department of Census and Statistics, *Sri Lanka Labour Force Survey, 1992: Final Report* (Colombo, February 1995).

Data from censuses and labour-force sample surveys indicate that while there is no significant difference in the overall labour-force participation rates of males between urban and rural areas, the rate for rural females is considerably higher than that for urban females. For example, Labour Force Survey data for the first quarter of 1995 show that the urban male rate of 65.9 per cent was only 2.6 percentage points higher than the corresponding rural rate, but the rural female rate of 33.7 per cent was 8.2 percentage points or a third more than the urban female rate (table 74).

Table 74. Labour-force participation rate by sex and residence: 1963-1995

Year and data source	Sri Lanka		Urban		Rural	
	Male	Female	Male	Female	Male	Female
1963 census	69.2	20.0	68.8	14.2	69.3	21.4
1971 census	68.5	26.0	68.9	21.1	68.3	27.4
1981 census	64.8	23.1	63.8	20.9	65.1	23.7
1985/86 Labour Force Survey[a]	68.6	32.6	67.2	26.8	68.8	31.0[b]
1995 Labour Force Survey[a]	63.8	32.1	65.9	25.8	63.3	33.7

Source: Department of Census and Statistics.

[a] Excluding Northern and Eastern provinces.

[b] Excluding the estate sector.

The significantly higher female labour-force participation rate in rural compared with urban areas is due to a number of factors. In the rural areas, there is a tendency to report women in farm households as unpaid family workers in agriculture. For instance, at the 1971 census, of the 90,528 females reported as unpaid family workers, as many as 88,333, or 97.6 per cent, were in rural areas, and nearly 88 per cent of the rural female unpaid family workers were enumerated as engaged in agriculture and related industry. Further, the opportunities for self-employment are greater in rural than in urban areas. A more significant reason is that the rural areas also include the estate sector in which, as noted earlier, the level of female labour-force participation is light. In fact, according to the 1985/86 Labour Force Survey, the female labour-force participation rate in the estate sector was 65.4 per cent, compared with 1.0 per cent in rural areas, excluding the estate sector.

4. Employed labour force

The economically active population or labour force includes both the employed and the unemployed persons. According to the definition adopted in the Sri Lanka Labour Force Surveys, employed persons are those who, during the reference period, worked as paid employees, employers, own-account workers (self-employed), or unpaid family workers. Also included are persons who had a job but were temporarily absent from work for such reasons as vacation, ill-health, bad weather or labour-management disputes.

The numerical distribution of the labour force by activity status, that is, employed or unemployed, and by sex for various years is shown in annex table E.1. The percentage distribution of the labour force by employment status and sex derived from data in annex table E.1 is given in table 75.

It will be noted from table 75 that since 1971 the proportion of the labour force reported as being employed has been lower among females than among males, and that this proportion for females is about 10-12 percentage points lower than that for males, according to the Labour Force Surveys of 1985/86, 1982, 1992 and 1996. Thus, in Sri Lanka, not only is the female labour-force participation rate considerably lower than the male rate, but the proportion of the labour force enumerated as employed is also significantly less than that for males.

The age-specific employment rates by sex for selected years are given in table 76.

It is evident from table 76 that the employment rate for females is significantly higher than the male rate at the youngest age group,

Table 75. Percentage distribution of the labour force by activity status and gender: 1963-1996

| Year and data source | Labour-force/activity status | | | | | | | | |
| | Employed | | | Unemployed | | | All statuses | | |
	Both sexes	Male	Female	Both sexes	Male	Female	Both sexes	Male	Female
1963 census	92.3	92.6	90.9	7.7	7.4	9.1	100.0	100.0	100.0
1971 census	81.3	85.7	68.9	18.7	14.3	31.1	100.0	100.0	100.0
1981 census	82.1	86.7	68.7	17.9	13.3	31.3	100.0	100.0	100.0
1985/86 Labour Force Survey	85.9	89.2	79.2	14.1	10.8	20.8	100.0	100.0	100.0
1992 Labour Force Survey[a]	85.5	89.3	77.8	14.5	10.7	22.2	100.0	100.0	100.0
1995 Labour Force Survey[a]	87.5	91.2	80.3	12.5	8.8	19.7	100.0	100.0	100.0
1996 Labour Force Survey[a]	88.7	92.0	82.4	11.3	8.0	17.6	100.0	100.0	100.0

Sources: Department of Census and Statistics, reports of the censuses of population and housing of 1963, 1971 and 1981; and reports of the Sri Lanka Labour Force Surveys of 1985/86, 1992, 1995 and 1996.

[a] Excluding Northern and Eastern provinces.

Table 76. Employment rates of the labour force by age group and sex: 1981, 1985/86 and 1992

Age group	1981 population census			1985/86 Labour Force Survey			1992 Labour Force Survey		
	Both sexes	Male	Female	Both sexes	Male	Female	Both sexes	Male	Female
10-14	57.3	56.5	59.2	90.4	68.3	88.1	80.7	75.2	88.6
15-19	56.6	60.4	48.1	68.3	71.4	62.2	58.5	61.6	53.6
20-24	65.2	72.4	49.6	69.6	76.7	57.5	65.7	72.7	54.4
25-29	78.9	86.0	61.5	83.3	89.4	72.3	81.1	87.5	68.9
30-34	87.5	92.6	73.2	89.8	93.1	83.3	90.4	94.5	82.0
35-39	92.1	95.4	82.6	94.3	95.4	92.1	94.5	95.9	92.1
40-44	95.1	96.7	89.9	94.5	94.6	94.3	97.0	97.8	95.1
45-49	96.7	97.4	94.2	96.4	96.9	95.4	97.6	98.0	96.6
50-54	97.4	97.8	95.8	97.8	97.9	97.7	98.4	98.1	99.6
55-59	97.7	98.0	96.2	95.4	94.8	97.7	98.4	98.3	98.7
60+	97.2	97.6	93.8	97.2	98.0	94.0	99.1	99.1	99.4
All ages 10+	82.1	86.7	68.7	85.9	89.2	79.2	89.4	89.3	77.8

Source: Department of Census and Statistics.

10-14 years, according to the censuses as well as Labour Force Surveys. For instance, in 1992, the employment rate for females aged 10-14 years (88.6 per cent) was about 13 percentage points higher than the corresponding rate for males (75.2 per cent). The 1992 Labour Force Survey also showed that while at ages 15-49 the male rates were significantly higher than the female rates, at ages 50 and over the rates were slightly higher for females than for males. Thus, the chances of being employed are greater for females than for males at the youngest and older age groups. It will also be noted from table 76 that employment rates of 95 per cent or higher were reported for men at ages 35 and older, and for women at ages 40 and above, in the 1992 Labour Force Survey.

The percentage distribution of the employed labour force by broad industrial sectors indicates that in 1981, as well as in 1995, the largest proportion among employed males as well as employed females were engaged in the agricultural sector (which comprises agriculture, forestry, hunting and fishing). However, during this 14-year period, there was a decline in the proportion of persons employed in the agricultural sector, in conformity with the general trends in the country. Yet in 1995, a higher proportion among females (41.5 per cent) than

males (34.4 per cent) continued to be engaged in this sector (table 77).

It is also evident from table 77 that, in 1981, the second largest proportion of employed males as well as females was engaged in the service sector, while the third largest proportion among employed females was in the manufacturing sector, and that among employed males was in the transport sector. But by 1995, the pattern of industrial attachment had changed significantly, with the second largest proportion of employed females being absorbed in the manufacturing sector, and the service sector being the avenue of employment for the third largest proportion among employed females. Between 1981 and 1991, there was an increase in the share of employed females in two other sectors, trade and finance.

The dramatic increase in the proportion of employed females absorbed in the manufacturing sector during the past 14 years has largely been due to the establishment of many industrial units in the country's export promotion zones, which have continued to employ a higher proportion of women than men. Available data indicate that in 1992 about 91 per cent of semi-skilled workers, 73 per cent of the unskilled workers and 89 per cent of the trainees in the three export promotion zones

Table 77. Percentage distribution of employed persons aged 10 years and over by major industrial sector and sex: 1981 and 1995

Major industrial groups	1981 population census			1995 Labour Force Survey		
	Both sexes	Male	Female	Both sexes	Male	Female
Agriculture, hunting, fishing and forestry	45.2	43.5	52.0	37.3	35.4	41.5
Mining and quarrying	0.9	0.9	0.3	1.1	1.3	0.4
Manufacturing	10.1	9.8	11.3	16.3	11.3	27.1
Electricity and gas	0.4	0.4	0.1	0.5	0.7	–
Construction	3.0	3.7	0.6	5.7	7.7	1.1
Trade, restaurants and hotels	10.5	12.1	4.4	10.4	12.8	5.3
Transport and communications	4.8	5.8	1.0	4.6	6.3	0.9
Finance, insurance, real estate	1.1	1.1	1.0	1.7	1.6	2.1
Community, social and personal services	14.5	12.2	23.3	16.8	15.7	19.4
Activity not classified	9.4	10.2	6.0	5.6	7.2	2.2
All industrial sectors	100.0	100.0	100.0	100.0	100.0	100.0

Sources: Department of Census and Statistics, 1981 Population and Housing Census, and 1995 (First Quarter) Labour Force Survey.

were women. Further, women constitute 90 per cent of the workers in the garment industries.

The percentage distribution of employed persons by employment status is given in table 78. The majority of employed males as well as employed females work as paid employees; this proportion has generally been higher among females than among males. According to the 1995 (First Quarter) Labour Force Survey, nearly 68 per cent of employed females as against 60 per cent of employed males were

Table 78. Percentage distribution of employed persons aged 10 years and over by employment status and sex: 1981, 1985/86, 1991 and 1995

Year and gender	Employment status				
	Employer	Employee	Own-account worker	Unpaid family worker	All statuses
1981					
Both sexes	2.2	65.8	28.4	3.6	100.0
Male	2.4	62.3	32.5	2.8	100.0
Female	1.2	79.4	12.9	6.5	100.0
1985/86					
Both sexes	2.3	58.5	26.0	13.2	100.0
Male	2.8	58.3	29.7	9.2	100.0
Female	0.9	59.0	17.4	22.7	100.0
1991 (First Quarter)[a]					
Both sexes	1.9	59.8	27.1	11.2	100.0
Male	2.6	59.9	31.7	5.8	100.0
Female	0.5	59.6	18.0	21.8	100.0
1995 (First Quarter)[a]					
Both sexes	2.5	62.4	26.2	8.9	100.0
Male	3.1	60.0	31.2	5.7	100.0
Female	1.1	67.6	15.1	16.2	100.0

Sources: Department of Census and Statistics, Population and Housing Census, 1981; and Sri Lanka Labour Force Surveys of 1985/86, 1991 (First Quarter) and 1995 (First Quarter).

[a] Excluding Northern and Eastern provinces.

engaged as paid employees. While the second largest proportion of females was employed as unpaid family workers, among males the second largest proportion was self-employed or own-account workers. In 1995, the proportion of self-employed males was more than double that for females, while the proportion of unpaid family workers among females was nearly three times that among males.

It is also evident from table 78 that, while the proportion of the male employed labour force engaged as paid employees increased only very slightly, from 58.3 per cent in 1985/86 to 60.0 per cent in 1995, that of employed females rose substantially, from 59.0 to 67.6 per cent, during the same 10-year period. Available information (not included in table 78) also indicates that nearly half of the jobs into which females were absorbed as paid employees were of a casual nature. The active promotion of self-employment as a panacea for unemployment had resulted in the proportion of self-employed or own-account workers increasing from 12.9 per cent in 1981 to 18.0 per cent is 1991. However, data from the 1995 Labour Force Survey indicate a decline in this proportion to 15.1 per cent, presumably because women now prefer casual paid employment to self-employment.

The proportion of employed women engaged as unpaid family workers more than trebled, from 6.5 per cent in 1981 to 22.7 per cent in 1985/86, but thereafter decreased to 16.2 per cent in 1995. The decline in this proportion over the past 10 years could be attributed to the increased level of educational attainment among women and expanding opportunities for paid employment outside the home. Further, in 1995, only 2.5 per cent of all employed persons were reported as employees, the proportion for males (3.1 per cent) being about three times that for females (1.1 per cent).

Data from the 1995 Sri Lanka Labour Force Survey show that among currently employed persons, a higher proportion of males than females worked longer hours in their main job during the reference week; nearly 68 per cent of the males compared with 64 per cent

of the females worked 40 or more hours a week, while 23.7 per cent of the females compared with 19.1 per cent of the currently employed males worked less than 30 hours a week (table 79).

Table 79. Percentage distribution of currently employed persons by hours per week actually worked at the main job and by gender: 1995

Hours per week	Both sexes	Male	Female
0-9	6.75	6.34	7.66
10-19	4.87	4.33	6.08
20-29	8.92	8.43	10.00
30-39	12.72	13.04	12.03
40-49	38.21	36.30	42.44
50+	28.52	31.56	21.80
Total	100.00	100.00	100.00

Source: Department of Census and Statistics, *Quarterly Report of the Sri Lanka Labour Force Survey: First Quarter, 1995* (Colombo, August 1995).

5. Unemployed persons

As noted earlier, the labour force comprises both the employed and the unemployed persons. For purposes of labour-force enumerations, persons who were available and looking for work and had no employment during the reference period were considered as unemployed.

Data from censuses and Labour Force Surveys indicate that the overall unemployment rate or proportion of the unemployed to the total labour force had increased sharply from 7.7 per cent in 1963 to 18.7 per cent in 1971, thereafter declining to 11.3 in 1996. While the trend for males is similar to the overall pattern, the female unemployment rate rose even more sharply, from 9.1 per cent in 1963 to 31.1 per cent in 1971, remaining at this level until 1981 before decreasing to 17.6 per cent in 1996. The available data also show that the female unemployment rate has consistently been at least double the male rate since 1971. In 1995, the female unemployment rate of 17.6 per cent was exactly double the rate of 8.8 per cent reported for males (see table 75).

The percentage distribution of the unemployed by age group and sex given in table 80 shows that unemployment is by and large a problem affecting young adults, with nearly 81 per cent of unemployed females and 82 per cent of unemployed males in 1962 being concentrated at ages 15-27 years.

A more reliable measure of the incidence and severity of the unemployment problem is the age-specific unemployment rate. These rates, based on the data of the 1985/86, 1990 and 1995 Labour Force Surveys, are shown in table 81. It will be noted that in 1985/86 and 1990, the highest rates of unemployment were recorded at ages 20-24 years, followed by ages 15-19 and 25-29 for females, and at ages 15-19 followed by 20-24 years for males. In 1990, a little over half of the females aged 20-24 years and more than a third of the females aged 15-19 years were enumerated as unemployed. According to the 1995 Labour Force Survey,

Table 80. Percentage distribution of unemployed persons by age group and sex: 1971-1992

Age group	1971 census		1981 census		1985/86 Labour Force Survey		1992 Labour Force Survey	
	Male	Female	Male	Female	Male	Female	Male	Female
10-14	3.5	3.6	4.5	2.2	1.7	0.5	1.0	0.3
15-19	26.9	21.7	28.0	19.2	25.6	18.6	24.5	18.0
20-24	35.7	34.8	33.5	34.9	34.5	38.9	40.7	41.4
25-29	14.2	17.6	16.0	22.0	13.9	21.2	16.4	21.1
30-34	5.8	7.5	8.0	11.9	7.9	10.5	6.7	10.6
35-39	3.9	4.5	3.6	5.4	4.8	4.3	4.2	4.7
40-44	2.7	2.8	2.2	2.3	4.2	2.4	2.4	2.2
45-49	2.2	2.3	1.5	1.0	2.1	1.6	1.7	1.3
50-54	1.6	1.7	1.1	0.5	1.3	0.6	1.2	0.1
55-59	1.3	1.3	0.7	0.3	2.6	0.3	0.8	0.2
60+	2.3	2.2	1.1	0.3	1.3	1.2	0.6	0.1
Total	100.0	100.0	100.0	100.0	100.0	100.0	100.0	100.0

Source: Department of Census and Statistics.

Table 81. Age-specific unemployment rates by sex: Labour Force Surveys of 1985/86, 1990 and 1995

Age group	1985/86			1990			1995		
	Both sexes	Male	Female	Both sexes	Male	Female	Both sexes	Male	Female
10-14	9.5	11.9	5.6	11.1	6.3	16.6	–	–	–
15-19	31.7	28.6	27.8	29.9	23.4	38.8	36.5	31.1	45.6
20-24	30.4	23.3	42.5	34.8	22.5	50.5	28.3	21.4	38.6
25-29	16.7	10.6	27.7	17.2	10.6	28.1	19.9	11.6	34.0
30-34	10.2	6.9	16.7	13.2	8.8	19.8	6.8	4.9	10.8
35-39	5.7	4.6	7.9	5.5	2.3	10.1	7.2	4.7	11.2
40-44	5.5	5.4	5.4	4.1	3.9	4.5	4.9	4.3	5.8
45-49	3.6	3.1	4.5	1.4	0.4	3.2	2.2	2.4	1.7
50-54	2.2	2.1	2.3	3.7	1.3	10.5	–	–	–
55-59	4.6	5.2	2.3	0.4	0.1	1.1	2.4	2.3	2.5
60+	2.6	2.3	3.4	3.6	4.5	–	–	–	–
All ages	14.1	10.8	20.8	14.4	9.1	23.5	12.5	8.8	19.7

Source: Department of Census and Statistics.

the highest unemployment rates for both males and females were recorded at ages 15-19 years, followed by the 20-24 and 25-29 age groups.

It is also clear from table 81 that unemployment rates generally decrease with advancing age and that the rates for females are higher than the corresponding male rates at almost all ages, this difference being more marked at the younger age groups. For instance, in 1995, nearly 46 per cent of females aged 15-19 years were reported to be unemployed as against 31 per cent of the males, and at ages 20-24 the unemployment rate was about 39 per cent for females compared with only 21 per cent for males. Those marked gender differences reflect the fact that women experience greater difficulties than men in finding employment.

In Sri Lanka, as in most other developing countries of the region, unemployment is reported to be a problem affecting the educated persons. Data from three Labour Force Surveys conducted in 1988/86, 1994 and 1995 show that the vast majority of the unemployed in the country are those males and females who had either some secondary education or had successfully completed secondary or higher level of education. For instance, in 1995 nearly 97 per cent of the unemployed males and about 95 per cent of the unemployed females were those who had completed some grades at secondary level or had passed the GCE (Ordinary Level) or higher-level examinations. It is also

important to note that while about 30 per cent of unemployed females had successfully completed 12 years of schooling (GCE (Advanced Level)) or college/university education, this proportion among unemployed males was only 9.0 per cent in 1995 (table 82).

An analysis of unemployment rates by level of educational attainment of the unemployed (table 83) indicates that these rates rise with the increasing educational level for both males and females. For instance, in 1994, the unemployment rate for females rose sharply from 1.6 per cent in respect of those with no education to 10.2 per cent for women with 1-5 years of schooling and further to 29.6 per cent for those with GCE (Ordinary Level) and to 34.1 per cent for those with GCE (Advanced Level) and/or university degrees. With the exception of those with no schooling, female unemployment rates are significantly higher for females than for males, being at least twice the male rate for every level of educational attainment beyond 6-10 years of schooling. Thus, contrary to the general perception that education helps upward occupational mobility, educated Sri Lankan women experience greater difficulty in finding employment than their male counterparts.

Data from the Labour Force Surveys also indicate that the duration of unemployment or waiting period to obtain a job in the desired or preferred occupational category has, on the average, been longer for females than males.

Table 82. Percentage distribution of the unemployed by level of educational attainment and sex: 1985/86, 1994 and 1995

Level of educational attainment	1985/86		1994		1995	
	Male	Female	Male	Female	Male	Female
No schooling	4.9	4.0	1.4	0.7	0.2	2.7
School years 1-5 (Primary education)	17.9	10.8	14.9	9.0	2.9	2.6
School years 6-10 (Secondary incomplete)	52.3	40.9	52.2	39.1	58.1	35.5
GCE (Ordinary Level)	19.6	30.6	22.5	28.1	29.8	29.6
GCE (Advanced Level)	4.9	12.8	9.0	23.1	9.0	29.6
Degree and above	0.4	0.9	–	–	–	–
Total	100.0	100.0	100.0	100.0	100.0	100.0

Source: Department of Census and Statistics, Sri Lanka Labour Force Surveys of 1985/86, 1994 (First Quarter) and 1995 (First Quarter).

Table 83. Unemployment rates by educational level and sex: 1985/86 and 1994

Educational level	1985/86			1994		
	Both sexes	Male	Female	Both sexes	Male	Female
No schooling	6.1	7.7	4.8	2.5	3.7	1.6
School years 1-5	7.7	7.0	9.4	8.9	8.3	10.2
School years 6-8	11.2	9.5	16.5	12.7	9.6	21.2
School years 9-10	20.8	15.4	34.9			
GCE (Ordinary Level)	22.3	14.4	35.6	18.4	12.2	29.6
GCE (Advanced Level)	32.0	18.7	44.9			
Degree	6.3	3.3	10.2	25.2	14.7	34.1
Postgraduate degree	3.9	4.2	3.2			
All educational levels	14.1	10.8	20.8	13.6	9.9	20.8

Source: Department of Census and Statistics, Sri Lanka Labour Force Surveys of 1985/86 and 1994 (First Quarter).

For example, according to the data from the 1995 Labour Force Survey, 84.6 per cent of unemployed females as against 78.9 per cent of unemployed males had to wait for six months or more to obtain employment in the desired occupational category, and the proportion having to wait for a year or more was 76.0 per cent for females compared with 71.3 per cent for males (table 84).

It is also evident from table 84 that a significantly higher proportion of unemployed females than males had to wait for a year or longer to obtain employment in managerial, pro-fessional, clerical, sales and services, and craft and related occupations. Nearly all unemployed females desiring employment in managerial and sales and services occupations, and about 92 per cent desiring clerical occupations, had to wait for 12 months or more.

The foregoing analysis clearly indicates that unemployment is more of a problem among young, educated Sri Lankan women than among their male counterparts. Not only are unemployment rates considerably higher for females compared with males, but women also experience greater difficulties than males

Table 84. Percentage distribution of unemployed persons by duration of unemployment and sex for various occupations desired: 1995

Occupation desired	Less than six months			Six to less than twelve months			Twelve months and over			Total		
	Both sexes	Male	Female	Both sexes	Male	Female	Both sexes	Male	Female	Both sexes	Male	Female
Managerial	–	–	–	–	–	–	100.0	–	100.0	100.0	–	100.0
Professional	9.9	43.5	8.6	5.4	5.6	5.4	84.7	51.0	86.0	100.0	100.0	100.0
Technical	11.6	15.0	9.8	22.6	–	34.1	65.9	85.0	56.1	100.0	100.0	100.0
Clerical	10.7	20.1	2.6	4.1	2.3	5.7	85.2	77.6	91.8	100.0	100.0	100.0
Sales and services	37.0	49.5	–	–	–	–	63.0	50.5	100.0	100.0	100.0	100.0
Agricultural and fishery	–	–	–	–	–	–	–	–	–	–	–	–
Craft and related	24.0	27.7	20.7	10.5	14.0	7.2	65.5	58.3	72.1	100.0	100.0	100.0
Plant and machine operator	35.0	14.9	56.0	–	–	–	65.0	85.2	44.0	100.0	100.0	100.0
Elementary occupations	11.7	13.6	1.2	3.1	–	20.2	85.2	86.4	78.7	100.0	100.0	100.0
Others	17.5	12.7	24.1	15.1	16.4	13.3	67.4	70.9	62.6	100.0	100.0	100.0
All occupations	18.0	21.1	15.3	8.2	7.6	8.6	73.8	71.3	76.0	100.0	100.0	100.0

Source: Department of Census and Statistics, *Quarterly Report of the Sri Lanka Labour Force Survey: First Quarter, 1995* (Colombo, August 1995).

A dash = negligible.

with equivalent qualifications in securing the jobs they desire. It would therefore appear that gender role perceptions continue to have an impact on the level and pattern of the economic participation of men and women in the country. As noted earlier, the general perception that women are not "breadwinners" but are only "secondary earners" continues to result in the marginalization of women in the economic life of the country.

6. Persons not in the labour force

According to data from censuses and Labour Force Surveys presented in annex table E.1, a very substantial proportion of persons in the working ages 10 years and over are actually not economically active or in the labour force, the proportion for both sexes combined varying from 50 to 55 per cent, depending on the data source. For instance, the First Quarter 1995 Labour Force Survey showed that nearly 52 per cent of all persons aged 10 years and over were not in the labour force, the proportion for females (68 per cent) being nearly double that for males (36 per cent).

An analysis of the persons aged 10 years and over currently not in the labour force by age groups indicates that in 1995 nearly 54 per cent of these persons were below 30 years of age, but this proportion for males (70.2 per cent) was considerably higher than the 45.1 per cent reported for females (table 85). In other words, nearly 55 per cent of the females aged 10 years and over who did not enter the labour force were aged 30 years and over. Thus, the lower overall labour force participation of females could to a large extent be attributed to the fact that over half of the women above 30 years of age were enumerated as economically not active.

At the 1995 Labour Force Survey, the important reason reported by the largest proportion of persons for currently not being in the labour force was "engaged in studies" (42.0 per cent), followed by "household work" (37.0 per cent) and "retired" (14.7 per cent). These proportions, however, varied markedly between males and females as well as across various age groups. The majority of the males (64.0 per cent) reported "engaged in studies" as the reason for being not economically active, while for the majority of the females (54.4 per cent) household work was the reason. Being retired was a more important reason for males (22.4 per cent) than for females (10.6 per cent) for not being in the labour force (table 86).

Table 85. Numerical and percentage distribution of persons aged 10 years and over currently not in the labour force by age group and sex: first quarter, 1995

Age group	Both sexes		Male		Female	
	Number	Percentage	Number	Percentage	Number	Percentage
10-14	1 705 798	25.67	857 134	37.66	848 664	19.43
15-19	1 206 853	18.16	597 706	26.26	609 147	13.94
20-24	368 546	5.54	110 846	4.87	257 700	5.90
25-29	288 049	4.34	32 924	1.45	255 125	5.84
30-34	328 002	4.94	9 481	0.42	318 521	7.29
35-39	310 685	4.68	20 088	0.88	290 597	6.65
40-44	354 518	5.34	25 049	1.10	329 469	7.54
45-49	288 261	4.34	38 001	1.67	250 260	5.73
50-54	291 712	4.39	29 025	1.28	262 687	6.01
55-59	322 725	4.86	87 290	3.84	235 435	5.39
60+	1 179 498	17.75	468 228	20.57	711 270	16.28
All ages 10+	6 644 647	100.00	2 275 772	100.00	4 368 875	100.0

Source: Department of Census and Statistics, *Quarterly Report of the Sri Lanka Labour Force Survey: First Quarter, 1995* (Colombo, August 1995).

Table 86. Percentage distribution of persons aged 10 years and over currently not in the labour force, by reason and by age group and sex: first quarter, 1995

Age group	Engaged in studies			Household work			Disabled or infirm			Retired			Other reasons			All reasons		
	Both sexes	Male	Female	Both sexes	Male	Female	Both sexes	Male	Female	Both sexes	Male	Female	Both sexes	Male	Female	Both sexes	Male	Female
10-14	95.2	95.6	94.7	3.3	3.1	3.5	0.2	0.1	0.4	..	..	..	1.3	1.2	1.4	100.0	100.0	100.0
15-19	83.8	89.8	77.9	8.9	2.6	15.0	1.2	1.7	0.8	..	..	..	6.1	5.9	6.3	100.0	100.0	100.0
20-24	36.3	80.1	17.5	53.0	3.5	74.4	3.0	9.5	0.1	..	..	..	7.7	6.8	8.0	100.0	100.0	100.0
25-29	6.7	32.7	3.3	88.4	62.2	91.8	0.4	..	0.4	..	..	..	4.6	5.1	4.5	100.0	100.0	100.0
30-34	0.1	1.1	0.1	90.4	..	93.1	2.7	..	2.8	..	..	..	6.8	98.9	4.0	100.0	100.0	100.0
35-39	..	..	..	89.5	22.7	94.1	3.0	9.0	2.6	0.5	7.9	..	7.0	60.4	3.3	100.0	100.0	100.0
40-44	..	..	..	87.2	0.4	93.8	6.2	28.0	4.6	1.9	26.4	0.1	4.6	45.2	1.6	100.0	100.0	100.0
45-49	0.2	0.5	0.1	78.9	..	90.9	8.6	54.2	1.6	8.9	30.0	5.7	3.4	15.3	1.7	100.0	100.0	100.0
50-54	0.6	..	0.6	83.0	11.7	90.9	1.9	18.6	..	12.3	60.1	7.0	2.3	9.6	1.5	100.0	100.0	100.0
55-59	..	..	..	53.3	6.7	70.6	9.2	29.0	1.9	32.2	53.8	24.2	5.3	10.5	3.3	100.0	100.0	100.0
60+	..	..	..	27.3	0.9	44.7	2.3	3.5	1.6	67.9	91.0	52.7	2.5	4.6	1.0	100.0	100.0	100.0
All ages 10+	42.0	64.0	30.5	37.0	3.7	54.4	2.4	4.3	1.4	14.7	22.4	10.6	3.9	5.6	3.0	100.0	100.0	100.0

Source: Department of Census and Statistics, *Quarterly Report of the Sri Lanka Labour Force Survey: First Quarter, 1995* (Colombo, August 1995).

Two dots (..) = negligible.

As is to be expected, the most important reason for young persons not being in the labour force is that they are engaged in studies; this reason was reported by about 95 per cent of males and females aged 10-14 years, and about 90 per cent of males and 80 per cent of females aged 15-19 years at the 1995 Labour Force Survey. Over 90 per cent of females at ages 25-54 years did not participate in the labour force as they had to attend to household chores. At older ages, 60 and over, being retired was the reason for which 91 per cent of the males and about 53 per cent of the females were not in the labour force (table 86).

7. Overseas employment

Sri Lanka has only a brief history of labour migration for employment outside the country. With the exception of a small stream of Sri Lankan Tamils, mainly from the Jaffna peninsula, who migrated to Malaysia during the first half of this century when both countries were British colonies, very few Sri Lankans had emigrated overseas in the past. On the other hand, Sri Lanka had been receiving external migrants, mostly South Indian Tamils, since the middle of the last century to work as indentured labourers on the plantations, but this migration, which consisted of both males and females, came to a halt when Sri Lanka achieved independence in 1948.

However, starting in the late 1960s, Sri Lanka experienced a new form of emigration of its nationals, that of highly qualified professionals for employment mainly in the developed countries, such as Australia, the United Kingdom of Great Britain and Northern Ireland and the United States of America, and to countries in East and West Africa. These migrant streams, which comprised a few thousand annually, consisted largely of males. However, in recent decades there has been an increasing outflow of middle-level skilled workers as well as unskilled workers to work in oil-rich countries and other developed Asian countries, where the demand for such labour has been rising over the years. Available data also indicate that an increasing proportion of the Sri Lankan worker emigrants has been women. For instance, according to data maintained by the Sri Lanka Bureau of Foreign Employment, of a total of 422,416 Sri Lankans who left the country between 1988 and 1995 for overseas employment through licensed sources, as many as 295,792, or 70 per cent, were women, and the relative share of women in total overseas labour migration increased steadily from 54.9 per cent in 1988 to 79.9 per cent in 1995 (table 87).

While comprehensive data on the total number of Sri Lankans who had left the country for employment in foreign countries over

Table 87. Sri Lankan nationals emigrating as migrant workers, by sex: 1988-1995

Year	Number of emigrating workers[a/]			Percentage female
	Both sexes	**Male**	**Female**	
1988	18 428	8 309	10 119	54.9
1989	24 724	8 680	16 044	64.9
1990	42 625	15 377	27 248	63.9
1991	65 128	21 516	43 612	67.0
1992	44 652	15 493	29 159	65.3
1993	48 753	17 153	31 600	64.8
1994	60 167	16 371	43 796	72.8
1995	117 939	23 725	94 214	79.9
Total	422 416	126 624	295 792	70.0

Source: Sri Lanka Bureau of Foreign Employment, cited in Department of Census and Statistics, *Changing Role of Women in Sri Lanka* (Colombo, January 1997).

[a/] Migration through licensed sources only.

the past few decades are not available, estimates based on information available from embarkation cards surrendered to emigration authorities at exit points, as well as information provided by employment agencies, indicate that as of 1996, the cumulative number of Sri Lankans working abroad amounted to about 550,000, of whom 378,500, or about 69 per cent, were women. These estimates also indicate that about 480,000, or 87 per cent of all Sri Lankan workers, are concentrated in the Middle East countries (table 88).

As noted earlier, the female dominance in temporary migration for overseas employment increased dramatically, from about 55 per cent of the total outflow in 1988 to about 80 per cent in 1995 (see table 87). This sharp increase has largely been due to a rise in the number of women leaving the country to work as housemaids. An analysis of the data on temporary migrant workers by occupational level for the period 1988-1995 indicates that of the 295,792 women emigrant workers, as many as 240,675, or 81.4 per cent, were housemaids, and that housemaids also constituted about 57 per cent of the emigrant workers during this period. Skilled and unskilled workers constituted only 18 per cent among all female emigrant

workers as compared with 86.5 per cent among male emigrant workers (table 89).

A classification by destination of the 240,675 Sri Lankan women emigrating to work as housemaids in 1988-1955 (table 90) shows that the vast majority (96.5 per cent) moved to Middle East countries where, over the years, it has become a symbol of high social status to hire a housemaid from abroad. The predominance of Sri Lankan maids in Arab households is largely due to the fact that Sri Lanka is the only South Asian country not to have banned the recruitment of women as foreign domestic workers. Within the Middle East region, Saudi Arabia is the most popular destination, followed by Kuwait and the United Arab Emirates. Among countries in other regions, Singapore employs the largest number of housemaids from Sri Lanka.

An analysis of 130,027 Sri Lankans recruited through various sources for overseas employment and emigrating through the airports in 1994 showed that 108,698, or 83.6 per cent, of these emigrant workers were women. Among the women worker emigrants, nearly 91 per cent were in the prime working ages, below 40 years, and 79 per cent were

Table 88. Estimated stock of Sri Lankan overseas contract workers by country of employment and gender: 1996

Country of employment	Estimated stock of Sri Lankan workers			Percentage female
	Both sexes	Male	Female	
Saudi Arabia	200 000	90 000	110 000	55.0
Kuwait	85 000	15 000	70 000	82.4
United Arab Emirates	75 000	15 000	60 000	80.0
Lebanon	25 000	1 000	24 000	96.0
Oman	25 000	5 000	20 000	80.0
Bahrain	20 000	5 000	15 000	75.0
Jordan	20 000	5 000	15 000	75.0
Qatar	15 000	5 000	10 000	66.7
Other Middle East countries	15 000	5 000	10 000	66.7
Italy	15 000	5 000	10 000	66.7
Far East countries	25 000	5 000	20 000	80.0
African countries	15 000	12 500	2 500	16.7
ASEAN countries	15 000	3 000	12 000	80.0
All countries	550 000	171 500	378 500	68.8

Source: Sri Lanka Bureau of Foreign Employment, cited in Department of Census and Statistics, *Changing Role of Women in Sri Lanka* (Colombo, January 1997).

Table 89. Sri Lankan nationals emigrating as temporary labour migrants[a/], by occupational category and sex: 1988-1995

Occupational level	Both sexes		Male		Female		Percentage female
	Number	Percentage	Number	Percentage	Number	Percentage	
Professional	1 759	0.4	1 677	1.3	82	..	4.7
Middle level	6 668	1.6	6 032	4.8	636	0.2	9.5
Clerical and related	10 704	2.5	9 316	7.4	1 388	0.5	13.0
Skilled	94 278	22.3	57 103	45.1	37 175	12.6	39.4
Unskilled	68 332	16.2	52 496	41.5	15 836	5.4	23.2
Housemaid	240 675	57.0	–	–	240 675	81.4	100.0
Total	422 416	100.0	126 624	100.0	295 792	100.0	70.0

Source: Sri Lanka Bureau of Foreign Employment, cited in Department of Census and Statistics, *Changing Role of Women in Sri Lanka* (Colombo, January 1997).

[a/] Including only migrants through licensed sources.

Table 90. Distribution of Sri Lankan women employed as housemaids in foreign countries by country of employment: 1988-1995

Country of employment	Number	Percentage
Middle East region	**232 324**	**96.5**
Bahrain	7 706	3.2
Jordan	6 457	2.7
Kuwait	74 656	31.0
Lebanon	4 192	1.7
Oman	8 582	3.6
Qatar	1 726	0.7
Saudi Arabia	94 574	39.3
United Arab Emirates	34 431	14.3
Other regions	**8 531**	**3.5**
Singapore	4 936	2.1
Other countries	3 415	1.4
Total	**240 675**	**100.0**

Source: Sri Lanka Bureau of Foreign Employment, cited in Department of Census and Statistics, *Changing Role of Women in Sri Lanka* (Colombo, January 1997).

and cultural mores of the country are conducive to the migration of older women; nearly 68 per cent of women workers emigrating in 1994 were between 25 and 44 years of age. Third, and more importantly, the economic pressures, such as the rising rate of inflation and unemployment, and reduction in social welfare subsidies, have acted as strong "push" factors for women to seek employment in foreign countries, even as domestic aides. In general, these women come from urban areas where unemployment rates are high and access to recruitment agencies is also relatively easy. A 1986 survey of 643 emigrant female workers revealed that nearly 45 per cent of them were seeking overseas employment because of insufficient income, while another about 15 per cent did so to provide for their children, and a further 10 per cent on account of their being currently in debt (table 92).

In general, Sri Lankan women who seek employment in foreign countries do so in order to augment the meagre incomes and resources of their families and to meet some basic needs for their family members. Their foreign earnings have to a large extent helped to improve the well-being of their family members, the long-term improvements being better housing and amenities. Case studies of returnee migrant domestic workers conducted by the Centre for Women's Research in 1987 show that in most cases the remittances have been used to meet consumption needs, but in some cases, after

married. The analysis also showed that only a third of the women emigrants had secured their employment with official clearance; others were recruited without official clearance or through personal contacts (table 91).

There are several reasons why an increasing number of Sri Lankan women emigrate to the Middle East for employment purposes. First, women spend relatively less money to obtain a job in the Gulf. Second, the social

Table 91. Sri Lankan nationals emigrating as temporary migrant workers by age group, marital status and source of employment: 1994[a/]

Background characteristics	Both sexes		Male		Female	
	Number	Percentage	Number	Percentage	Number	Percentage
All employees	**130 027**	**100.0**	**21 329**	**100.0**	**108 698**	**100.0**
Age group						
20 or less	6 291	4.8	570	2.7	5 721	5.3
21-25	23 705	18.2	4 872	22.8	18 833	17.3
26-30	27 636	21.3	5 428	25.4	22 208	20.4
31-35	34 258	26.3	4 299	20.2	29 959	27.6
36-40	25 426	19.6	3 360	15.8	22 066	20.3
41-45	10 361	8.0	1 954	9.2	8 407	7.7
46-50	2 168	1.7	749	3.5	1 419	1.3
51 and above	182	0.1	97	0.5	85	0.1
Marital status						
Unmarried	29 677	22.8	6 755	31.7	22 922	21.1
Married	100 350	77.2	14 574	68.3	85 776	78.9
Source of employment						
With official clearance	47 141	36.3	10 392	48.7	36 749	33.8
Without official clearance	50 904	39.1	4 555	21.4	46 349	42.6
Through personal contacts	31 982	24.6	6 382	29.9	25 600	23.6

Source: Sri Lanka Bureau of Foreign Employment, cited in Department of Census and Statistics, *Changing Role of Women in Sri Lanka* (Colombo, January 1997).

[a/] Based on an Airport Survey (excluding vacationers).

Table 92. Migrant workers by reason for seeking employment abroad and by sex: 1986

Reason for seeking employment in foreign countries	Male		Female	
	Number	Percentage	Number	Percentage
To accumulate savings	56	19.1	74	11.5
Insufficient income	107	36.5	287	44.6
To provide for children	16	5.5	96	14.9
Personal debt	10	3.4	62	9.6
Lack of employment opportunities	36	12.3	62	9.6
To gain experience	17	5.8	11	1.7
Domestic/personal crisis	51	17.4	51	7.9
Total	293	100.0	643	100.0

Source: Based on a survey carried out by the Marga Institute, 1986.

more than one contract, the families have been able to save and invest in a piece of land, build a house, or effect improvements to an existing house (table 93).

Table 93. Use of remittances by a sample of women worker migrants to the Middle East in two urban localities of Sri Lanka

Use of remittance	Weerapura		Palliveediya	
	Number	Percentage	Number	Percentage
For consumption	16	80.0	16	80.0
For children's education	3	15.0	1	5.0
To settle debts	1	5.0	2	10.0
For construction/ repair of house	8	40.0	–	–
To furnish the house	–	–	2	10.0
On mother's illness	–	–	1	5.0
For brother's wedding	–	–	1	5.0
For liquor and cigarettes	1	5.0	–	–
To purchase a motor cycle	1	5.0	–	–
Part has been saved	2	10.0	–	–
Whole amount has been saved	2	10.0	–	–
Not reported	–	–	2	10.0

Source: Centre for Women's Research.

Although the immediate family members have benefited from the remittances of their female members working overseas, many of the women themselves have had traumatic experiences in regard to their employment in a foreign environment. They have been exploited by recruitment agencies in Sri Lanka and by employers overseas. According to information available from the Sri Lanka Bureau of Foreign Employment, a total of 10,880 complaints were received from Sri Lankan women workers abroad between 1985 and 1990, and as many as 9,381, or 86 per cent, of these complaints were from women working in the domestic sector. Nearly 48 per cent of the complaints from women in the domestic sector and 45 per cent from women in the non-domestic sector related to harassment and the non-payment of wages (table 94).

Over the years, government labour policies have encouraged emigration as an alternative method of solving the country's unemployment problems, particularly female unemployment. The remittances of female migrant workers have also contributed significantly to the country's foreign exchange earnings and balance of payments. Available information also indicates that the existing demand for housemaids will continue, as domestic work is not an attractive occupation for nationals in the home countries. Consequent on this increased demand for female domestic labour, the dominant position of females in the total outflow of migrant workers from Sri Lanka is likely to be main-

tained in the near future. Hence, it is essential to take adequate measures to protect female migrant workers from exploitation and other traumatic experiences, including sexual harassment.

F. WOMEN IN PUBLIC LIFE

1. Women in politics

In Sri Lanka, women's involvement in the political life of the country dates back to 1981, when public-sprited men and women came forward to form the Ceylon National Congress to agitate for and obtain constitutional reforms from the British colonial power. Later, in 1927, a group of selected women made representations to the Donoughmore Commission for the grant of adult franchise to women, and universal franchise was granted to all citizens in 1931, thereby enabling women also to vote and participate in all aspects of political life.

Over the years, an increasing number and proportion of eligible women have been registering as voters and, except in the very backward and remote areas, the sex ratio of registered voters generally approximated that of the population. Estimates indicate that women constituted approximately 50 per cent of the 10.9 million registered voters at the 1994 parliamentary elections. A gender breakdown of registered voters actually voting at various elections held in the country is not available.

Table 94. Numerical and percentage distribution of complaints from Sri Lankan women working abroad, by nature of complaint and sector of employment: 1985-1990[a/]

Nature of complaint	Domestic sector		Non-domestic sector		All sectors	
	Number	Percentage	Number	Percentage	Number	Percentage
Harassment and non-payment of wages	4 491	47.9	377	25.2	4 868	44.7
Breach of contract	1 297	13.8	729	48.6	2 026	18.6
Lack of communication	2 602	27.7	156	10.4	2 758	25.3
Death/stranded	783	8.3	173	11.5	956	8.8
Others	208	2.2	64	4.3	272	2.5
Total	9 381	100.0	1 499	100.0	10 880	100.0

Source: Sri Lanka Bureau of Foreign Employment.

[a/] Data for 1990 only up to October 1990.

Nevertheless, based on the relatively high voter turnout at the elections (as for example, 81 per cent in 1965, 63.3 per cent in 1989 and 81 per cent in the 1994 parliamentary elections, and 75 per cent in the 1994 presidential elections), it is contended that not only has an increasing proportion of women gone to the polls but also the female voter turnout has been almost equal to that of men in recent years.

The high female voter turnout in Sri Lanka is due to a combination of several factors. As noted earlier, the literacy rate and educational attainment levels of Sri Lankan women are among the highest in the world. Second, owing to the effective media network, politics has today entered every Sri Lankan home and women are very knowledgeable about political developments in the country. Further, Sri Lankan women are very conscious of the power of their vote. In fact, it is the generally accepted view that the women's vote was a major factor in the complete rejection of the 1970-1977 government at the 1977 general elections, because it was the housewives, more than anyone else, who had to put up with the scarcity of essential commodities that had characterized the ousted regime.

Although women have been as conscious as men of the need to exercise their voting rights, their participation in national- as well as local-level politics as candidates at the various elections is quite low. There were no women candidates at the general elections to the First State Council held in 1931, the year in which women were granted the franchise, and only two women were among the 358 candidates contesting the general elections to the first Parliament of independent Sri Lanka in 1947. Available data (table 95) also show that women constituted less than 5 per cent of the total number of candidates contesting the national- as well as local-level elections during the past two decades.

The low proportion of women in the total number of candidates contesting elections has often been attributed to the leadership of political parties, which had for a long time been exclusively male. But that there is more to this than the antagonistic attitudes or prejudices of men is borne out by the fact that at the 1977 parliamentary elections, women constituted only 17 per cent of the candidates nominated by the Sri Lanka Freedom Party, which was led by a woman, as against 25 per cent of

Table 95. Numerical and percentage distribution of candidates contesting elections to Parliament, provincial councils and local authorities, by sex: 1977-1989

Legislature	Election year	Number of candidates contesting			
		Both sexes	Male	Female	Percentage female
Parliament					
Elections	1977	730	716	14	1.9
	1989	1 396	1 367	29	2.1
	1994	1 310	1 255	55	4.2
By-elections[a]	1977-1989	257	252	5	1.9
Provincial councils	1989	1 327	1 289	38	2.9
	1993	2 351	2 339	12	0.5
Local authorities					
Municipal councils	1987	641	619	22	3.4
	1991	1 152	1 108	44	3.8
Urban councils	1987	984	953	31	3.2
	1991	1 453	1 413	40	2.8
Pradeshiya Sabha	1987	7 198	7 065	133	1.8
	1991	13 385	13 060	325	2.4

Source: Department of Elections.

[a] There were 28 by-elections between 1977 and 1989.

the candidates contesting under the male-led United National party. It may also be noted that so far there have been no Muslim female candidates in any of the elections held in the country. The non-participation of Muslim women in politics is largely due to their relatively low levels of literacy as well as the conservative socio-cultural values of the Muslim community. Further, despite the fact that women constitute nearly half the voting population, no political party has made a conscious effort to woo women voters. Even at the 1977 general elections, held after International Women's Year 1975, only one of the party manifestos focused on women as a group.

Since only a very few women were nominated to contest the elections, women's representation in various legislative bodies has also been very low, with less than 5 per cent of the total members of any legislative organ at any one time. For instance, although the number of women members of Parliament, the highest legislative authority in the country, had almost trebled, from 4 in 1965 to 11 in 1994, their proportionate share less than doubled from 2.6 to 4.9 per cent during the same period owing to the increase in total membership (table 96). Thus, only 10 women were elected by popular vote to the National Parliament in 1994, despite

Table 96. Parliament membership by sex: 1965-1994

Year	Number of members			Percent-age female
	Both sexes	Male	Female	
1965	151[a]	147	4	2.6
1970	151[a]	145	6	4.0
1977	168	163	5[b]	3.0
1989	225	214	11[c]	4.9
1994	225	214	11[c]	4.9

Source: Department of Elections.

[a] Including 145 elected and 6 nominated members.

[b] When Parliament was dissolved in 1989, there were nine women members constituting 5.4 per cent of the total membership since five of them were appointed under election laws promulgated in terms of the 1979 Constitution, whereby a vacancy in Parliament is filled by appointment from a list of names submitted by different political parties and not through a by-election, as before.

[c] Ten elected and appointed from the National List.

63 years of women's franchise; a more than doubling of the female population during this period; universal free education for 46 years and the substantial increase in the female literacy rate and level of educational attainment; and Sri Lanka's achievement of having the world's first woman Prime Minister in 1960 and the country's first woman President in 1994.

In Sri Lanka, women are also very much underrepresented in provincial and various other local governing councils. In 1989, when elections were held for the first time to the newly created provincial councils, a smaller proportion of women was elected to these councils than to Parliament. Of the 437 provincial councillors elected in 1989, only 13, or approximately 3 per cent, were women. In 1991, the North East Provincial Council was dissolved, and of the 382 provincial councillors elected in 1993, only 12, or 3.1 per cent, were women. The proportion of women in other local bodies, such as municipalities, urban councils and Pradeshiya Sabhas, is still lower than in the provincial coucils (table 97).

Since women are grossly underrepresented in the local-level councils, they fail to be elected as heads of these councils. It will be noted from table 97 that there was only one woman mayor of municipality and three women chairpersons of Pradeshiya Sabhas in 1991, and that in 1994, there were no women holding any of the urban councils.

Reluctance on the part of political parties to nominate women as candidates is not the only or the main reason for the very low participation of women in legislative bodies. Besides the traditional constraints of childbearing and child-rearing, and the deep-rooted conviction that the woman's place is in the home and not the arena of public life, there was in the 1980s a stronger constraint that was largely responsible for the very low participation of women in politics. This was the violence and ruthlessness which had recently entered the political scene in Sri Lankan party politics during election time so that elections have been considered tough and dirty, involving character assassination and creating splits in families and in communities. This is a situation which neither the

Table 97. Women in local government councils: 1991 and 1994

Council and number of councils	Year	Councillors/members			Mayor/Chairman			Deputy Mayor/Vice-Chairman		
		Both sexes	Female	Percentage female	Both sexes	Female	Percentage female	Both sexes	Female	Percentage female
Municipalities										
10 councils	1991	192	6	3.1	10	1	10	10	–	–
1 council	1994	17	–	–	1	–	–	1	–	–
Urban councils										
33 councils	1991	280	7	2.5	3.3	–	–	33	1	3.0
2 councils	1994	17	–	–	2	–	–	2	–	–
Pradeshiya Sabha										
194 Sabhas	1991	2 754	33	1.2	194	3	1.5	194	1	0.5
37 Sabhas	1994	308	1	0.3	37	–	–	3.7	–	–

Sources: 1991 Report of the Commissioner of Elections for the year 1991, and table VIII of *Gazette Sri Lanka* of 25 March 1994.

Note: In 1991, elections were held for all provinces except North-East Province; and in 1994 elections were held for East Province.

women themselves (unless highly motivated), nor their families, would wish to face.

In this connection, it must be noted that since the time of the first State Council (1931), all women members of the national legislature have come from a politically influential background; either their natal or husbands' families have been deeply involved in political activities. Another conspicuous feature relating to most of these women parliamentarians is that they first enter the national legislature to fill the vacancy created by a close relative such as a husband, father or brother.

2. Women in militarized political movements

A recent phenomenon in Sri Lanka is the active participation of women in two militarized political movements. The Janatha Vimukthi Peramuna (JVP) in the southern Sinhala-speaking areas is a youth movement aimed at addressing the problems facing youth and creating a just society free of corruption, either through revolutionary moves against the democratically elected government or by participating in the democratic or electoral process. The Liberation Tigers of Tamil Eelam (LTTE) in the Tamil-speaking north and east is fighting for a separate homeland for the Tamil-speaking people of the country.

Women have participated actively in both the JVP and LTTE movements. Women cadres of LTTE are as well trained as men and participate in military activities, while young women and girls have been actively involved in JVP. Women have not only been part and parcel of these movements but have also been victims of violence at the hands of not only Eelamists and JVP but also the police and the army. In the north and east, women were mobilized en masse through Mothers' Fronts, which were among the first groups to protest against arbitrary arrests, assassinations and disappearances of young persons, chiefly males. Through demonstrations and fasts, the Mothers' Fronts act as pressure groups and as channels through which certain conditions and situations are brought to the attention of the public. Today, their stance has shifted from a political one to welfare work within the community.

The Mothers' Front in the south started just as violence and extrajudicial executions in the south were abating. Like their counterparts in the north and east, the Fronts in the south started initially as pressure groups against arbitrary arrests, assassinations and disappearances, but are now functioning as welfare groups within the community.

3. Women in decision-making positions

The very low and generally decreasing female participation in the established political structure and processes has resulted in marked gender imbalances at the highest decision-making levels. Available data indicate that there were no women appointed as ministers during the first Parliament in 1947. Since 1956, women have assumed responsibility as Cabinet ministers, although their numbers did not exceed two at any time. However, a larger number of women were appointed as non-Cabinet-level ministers, that is, either as deputy minister, state minister, district minister or project minister, as and when such ranks were created. Even today, with a woman President and a woman Prime Minister at the helm, only 2 of the 22 Cabinet ministers and 5 of the 30 deputy ministers are women (see table 98).

Although, as noted earlier, there are no legal barriers to the participation of women in education even at the highest academic and professional levels, and all occupations are open to women, their representation at the highest non-political decision-making levels is comparatively low. In Sri Lanka, the Permanent Secretaries (referred to as Secretaries) are the highest ranking non-political decision makers of the government. It will be noted from table 99 that since 1980 there were no women appointed to serve as Secretaries to Cabinet-level ministers, and in 1993 there were only seven women among the 55 non-Cabinet-level Secretaries.

Consequent on the policy of devolution of powers, provincial councils were established in 1988, and from that date all eight Chief Secretaries in the provinces have been men. In 1993,

Table 98. Participation of women at the ministerial level: 1980-1994

Year	Cabinet-level				Non-Cabinet-level			
	Both sexes	Male	Female	Percent-age female	Both sexes	Male	Female	Percent-age female
1980	26	25	1	3.8	39	39	–	–
1985	28	26	2	7.1	42	42	–	–
1990	26	25	1	3.8	52	47	5	9.6
1993	29	28	1	3.4	52	47	5	9.6
1994	22	20	2	9.1	30	25	5	16.7

Source: Office of the Parliament.

Table 99. Distribution of Secretary-level positions by level and sex: 1980, 1985 and 1993

Year	Cabinet-level				Non-Cabinet-level			
	Both sexes	Men	Women	Percent-age women	Both sexes	Men	Women	Percent-age women
1980	26	26	–	–	39	39	–	–
1985	29	29	–	–	52	49	3	5.8
1991	32	32	–	–	55	48	7	12.7

Source: Ministry of Public Administration.

the executive powers of the District Administration were decentralized from 25 districts to 306 divisions. There were only two women among the 25 District Secretaries in 1993.

Over the years, an increasing number of women have been recruited to the Sri Lanka Administrative Service; the number of women in various levels of this service increased from 117 in 1979 to 290 in 1993, with their relative share increasing from 7.6 to 17.1 per cent during the same period. However, most of the women are concentrated in the lowest level of this service; in 1993, nearly 59 per cent of all women in the Sri Lanka Administrative Service were in Class II-Grade 2, the corresponding proportion among males being only 43 per cent. Only about 13 per cent of officers in class I were women (see table 100).

The number of women recruited to the Sri Lanka Scientific Service also increased, from 26 in 1984 to 47 in 1995, with their proportionate share rising from 11.7 to 20.1 per cent during the 11-year period. As in the case of the Sri Lanka Administration Service, most women scientific officers are concentrated in the lowest level; in 1995 as many as 38, or 81 per cent, of the 47 female officers were in Class II-Grade 2 of this Service, and only about 10 per cent of the 29 officers in class I were women (table 101).

There has also been a steady increase in the number as well as the relative share of women in the Sri Lanka Planning Service; while the number of women increased markedly from 16 in 1979 to 306 in 1995, their proportionate share increased from 16.2 to 29.7 per

Table 100. Distribution of officers in the Sri Lanka Administrative Service by level and sex: 1979 and 1993

Level	1979				1993			
	Both sexes	Male	Female	Percent-age female	Both sexes	Male	Female	Percent-age female
Class I	165	162	3	1.8	445	389	56	12.6
Class II-Grade 1	345	326	19	5.5	477	414	63	13.2
Class II-Grade 2	1 035	940	95	9.2	777	606	171	22.0
Total	1 545	1 428	117	7.6	1 699	1 409	290	17.1

Source: Ministry of Public Administration.

Table 101. Distribution of members of the Sri Lanka Scientific Service by level and sex: 1984 and 1995

Level	1984				1995			
	Both sexes	Male	Female	Percent-age female	Both sexes	Male	Female	Percent-age female
Class I	25	25	–	–	29	26	3	10.3
Class II-Grade 1	44	38	6	13.6	55	49	6	10.9
Class II-Grade 2	154	134	20	13.0	150	112	38	25.3
Total	223	197	26	11.7	234	187	47	20.1

Source: Sri Lanka Scientific Service Board.

cent during the same period owing to the dramatic increase in the total cadre recruited to this service. As in the case of the Sri Lanka Administrative Service and the Sri Lanka Scientific Service, a vast majority of the women in the Planning Service (89.2 per cent) were concentrated in the lower rungs of this service in 1995. Among the 26 officers in Class I of the Sri Lanka Planning Service in 1995, only 3, or 11.5 per cent, were women (table 102).

The Sri Lanka Foreign or Overseas Service was a male-dominated service until 1958, when it was opened to women with university degrees. Since then several women have been recruited to the Service. However, in Sri Lanka, as in most other countries, practically all positions at the highest level of the diplomatic service, such as Ambassadors and High Commissioners, have traditionally been occupied by political appointees. It was only in recent

years that a certain number were being appointed from among senior and experienced members of the Foreign Service or even of the government services. The lower levels of the diplomatic positions are generally filled by members of the career diplomatic service.

Data from the Ministry of Foreign Affairs indicate that in 1980 there were only two women among the 26 Ambassadors and High Commissioners, but this number decreased to one in 1990; as at December 1993, there were no women Ambassadors or High Commissioners. Available data also indicate that no woman has so far been appointed as Permanent Representative or even as Deputy High Commissioner. At the lower diplomatic levels, the number as well as relative share of women has increased since 1980, and in 1993 women constituted about 16 per cent of the 79 positions at this level (table 103).

**Table 102. Distribution of officers in the Sri Lanka Planning Service by level and sex:
1979, 1988 and 1995**

Level	1979				1988				1995			
	Both sexes	Male	Female	Percentage female	Both sexes	Male	Female	Percentage female	Both sexes	Male	Female	Percentage female
Class I	–	–	–	–	2	2	–	–	26	23	3	11.5
Class II-Grade 1	5	4	1	20.0	84	68	16	19.0	138	108	30	21.7
Class II-Grade 2	94	79	15	16.0	92	72	20	21.7	866	593	273	31.5
Total	99	83	16	16.2	178	142	36	20.2	1 030	724	306	29.7

Source: Sri Lanka Planning Service Board.

Table 103. Representation of women in the foreign missions of Sri Lanka: 1980-1993

Year	Ambassadors/High Commissioners			Permanent Representatives			Deputy High Commissioners			Lower-level diplomatic positions		
	Both sexes	Female	Percentage female	Both sexes	Female	Percentage female	Both sexes	Female	Percentage female	Both sexes	Female	Percentage female
1980	26	2	7.7	2	–	–	1	–	–	55	6	10.9
1985	28	–	–	2	–	–	2	–	–	70	11	15.7
1990	33	1	3.0	2	–	–	4	–	–	73	11	15.1
1993	34	–	–	2	–	–	5	–	–	79	13	16.5

Source: Ministry of Foreign Affairs.

Although an increasing number of women are completing university courses and are being recruited to the university teaching staff, they are grossly underrepresented in management and decision-making positions in the various institutions of higher education. In 1991, no woman was functioning as vice-chancellor or registrar in any one of the nine universities in the country; only 35, or 17.3 per cent, of the 202 heads of departments, and 6, or about 7 per cent, of the 88 deans in the nine universities were women.

4. Women in government service

Over the years, an increasing number of women have been recruited for employment at various levels in government service, including the public, corporation and provincial sectors. During the 10 years from 1980 to 1990 alone, the number of women in government service increased by about 56 per cent, from 133,476 to 207,856, and their relative share from 22.3 to 29.7 per cent during the same period. In 1990, about 77 per cent of all women government employees were concentrated in the state and provincial sectors, while the remaining 23 per cent were employed in the semi-government or corporation sector, the corresponding proportions for men being about 53 and 47 per cent (table 104).

An analysis of all government employees in 1990 indicates that 58.2 per cent of all female employees, as against 13.9 per cent of male employees, were classified as professional, and females also constituted 63.8 per cent of professionals in government service. The very large proportion of females in the professional category is due to the fact that this group also includes government schools and paramedical personnel in government medical institutions, who are mostly females. The second largest proportion of female government employees was clerical workers (19.5 per cent): female clerks constituted 41.4 per cent of all clerical workers in 1990. Only about 11 per cent of the 9,048 senior officials and managers were women; women were also very much underrepresented in occupational groups such as craft and related workers, and machine operators and related workers (table 105).

5. Women in the judicial system

In recent decades, an increasing number of Sri Lankan women have taken up the study of law both at the Sri Lanka Law College and in the law faculties of the universities. Available data also show that the proportion of women in the total number passing out as attorneys from the Law College rose from 40 per

Table 104. Numerical and percentage distribution of government employees by sector and sex: 1980, 1985 and 1990

Year and sector	Both sexes		Male		Female	
	Number	Percentage	Number	Percentage	Number	Percentage
1980 Public sector	368 849	61.7	261 198	43.7	107 651	18.0
Corporation sector	228 531	38.3	202 706	33.9	25 825	4.3
All sectors	597 380	100.0	463 904	77.7	133 476	22.3
1985 Public sector	406 359	55.7	260 576	35.7	145 783	20.0
Corporation sector	322 617	44.3	277 517	38.1	45 100	6.2
All sectors	728 976	100.0	538 093	73.8	190 883	26.2
1990 State sector	198 425	28.3	161 887	23.1	36 538	5.2
Provincial public sector	222 584	31.8	99 892	14.3	122 692	17.5
Semi-government sector	279 583	39.9	230 957	33.0	48 626	6.9
All sectors	700 592	100.0	492 736	70.3	207 856	29.7

Source: Department of Census and Statistics, Censuses of Public and Corporation Sector Employment, 1980, 1985 and 1990.

Table 105. Numerical and percentage distribution of government employees by occupational group and sex: 1990

Year and sector	Both sexes		Male		Female		Percentage female
	Number	Percentage	Number	Percentage	Number	Percentage	
Senior officials and managers	9 048	1.3	8 035	1.6	1 013	0.5	11.2
Professionals	189 720	27.1	68 684	13.9	121 036	58.2	63.8
Technicians and associate professionals	83 854	12.0	66 245	13.4	17 609	8.5	21.0
Clerks	97 781	14.0	57 304	11.6	40 477	19.5	41.4
Services and sales workers	81 492	11.6	75 953	15.4	5 539	2.7	6.8
Agriculture and fishery workers	63	–	58	–	5	–	7.9
Craft and related workers	45 199	6.5	43 438	8.8	1 761	0.8	3.9
Machine operators and related workers	40 863	5.8	39 517	8.0	1 346	0.6	3.3
Elementary occupations	152 572	21.8	133 502	27.1	19 070	9.2	12.5
All occupational groups	700 592	100.0	492 736	100.0	207 856	100.0	29.7

Source: Department of Census and Statistics, Census of Public Sector and Corporation Sector Employment, 1990.

cent in 1985 to 44 per cent in 1992, and that the relative share of women in total enrolments in the law faculties had increased from 47.5 per cent in 1985/86 to 52.9 per cent in 1990/91; thus, during the academic year 1990/91 female students outnumbered males in the law faculties of the universities.

Consequent on the increase in the number of females qualifying as lawyers, there has been a rise in the number of women enrolled at the Bar or permitted to practise law in the country. Data from the Bar Association of Sri Lanka show that the number of women at the Bar had more than doubled, from 116 in 1995 to 288 in 1992, while their relative share improved from 40.1 to 48.6 per cent during this seven-year period (table 106).

Table 106. Men and women at the Bar: 1985 and 1992

Year	Number enrolled			Percent-age women
	Both sexes	Men	Women	
1985	289	173	116	40.1
1992	592	304	288	48.6

Source: Bar Association of Sri Lanka.

Over the years, an increasing number of women have become professional, practising lawyers and attorneys, with several of them accepting suitable positions in various government departments as well as in the Attorney General's Department as state prosecutors, state attorneys and state counsels. The first woman State Counsel was appointed in Sri Lanka in 1978. An increasing number of women have also been appointed to the country's judiciary. While in the past, the initial appointment of women to the judiciary was limited to the Juvenile Court, there are no barriers in regard to women's entry to the judiciary at any level of judicial office. The number as well as the relative share of women judges in the lower courts more than doubled between 1985 and 1993; nearly a quarter of the judges in district magistrate and primary courts are women (table 107).

The only woman judge of the High Court was appointed in 1988, and until 1993 there were no women functioning as judges of the Court of Appeal or in the Supreme Court.

6. Women in the armed forces

Women were first enlisted into the lowest ranks of the police force in 1953. Data from the Police Department indicate that although the number of women police increased more than fivefold from 197 in 1980 to 1,050 in 1993, their proportionate share increased only three-fold, from 1.2 to about 3.5 per cent, during the same period (table 108). Thus, even after 40 years of enlistment, women constitute a very small proportion of the country's police force. Women are also very much underrepresented in other defence forces, constituting about 1.0 per cent in the army, 2.7 per cent in the air force, and 2.0 per cent in the navy in 1993.

**Table 107. Judges in the lower courts,[a/]
by sex: 1985, 1990 and 1993**

Year	Number of judges			Percent-age women
	Both sexes	Men	Women	
1985	148	131	17	11.5
1990	162	131	31	19.1
1993	164	126	38	23.2

Source: Judicial Service Commission.

[a/] Including district magistrate and primary courts.

**Table 108. Distribution of police personnel,
by sex: 1980, 1985, 1990 and 1993**

Year	Number of judges			Percent-age women
	Both sexes	Men	Women	
1980	16 892	16 695	197	1.2
1985	20 095	19 585	510	2.5
1990	30 977	29 929	1 048	3.4
1993	30 407	29 357	1 050	3.5

Source: Police Department.

PART II

ANNEX TABLES

Table B.1 Land area, estimated mid-year population and population density by province and district: 1995

Province/district	Land area[a/]		Population		Density (persons per sq km)
	Square kilometres	Percentage of total area	Number (thousands)	Percentage of total population	
Western Province	3 631.9	5.6	4 656	25.7	1 282
Colombo	656.7	1.0	2 095	11.6	3 190
Gampaha	1 386.6	2.2	1 582	8.7	1 141
Kalutara	1 588.6	2.5	979	5.4	616
Central Province	5 620.1	8.7	2 296	12.7	409
Kandy	1 906.3	3.0	1 306	7.2	685
Matale	1 993.3	3.1	440	2.4	221
Nuwara Eliya	1 720.5	2.7	550	3.0	320
Southern Province	5 497.4	8.5	2 362	13.0	430
Galle	1 635.6	2.5	996	5.5	609
Matara	1 282.5	2.0	822	4.5	641
Hambantota	2 579.3	4.0	544	3.0	211
Northern Province	8 687.6	13.5	1 379	7.6	159
Jaffna	983.6	1.5	905	5.0	920
Kilinochchi	1 235.0	1.9	112	0.6	91
Mannar	1 985.2	3.1	141	0.8	71
Mullaitivu	2 516.9	3.9	100	0.6	40
Vavuniya	1 966.9	3.1	121	0.7	62
Eastern Province	9 635.3	14.9	1 305	7.2	135
Batticaloa	2 686.3	4.2	452	2.5	168
Ampara	4 318.2	6.7	522	2.9	121
Trincomalee	2 630.8	4.1	331	1.8	126
North-Western Province	7 826.2	12.1	2 135	11.8	273
Kurunegala	4 812.8	7.5	1 499	8.3	311
Puttalam	3 013.4	4.7	636	3.5	211
North-Central Province	10 258.5	15.9	1 103	6.1	108
Anuradhapura	7 034.3	10.9	763	4.2	108
Polonnaruwa	3 224.2	5.0	340	1.9	105
Uva Province	8 348.4	13.0	1 122	6.2	134
Badulla	2 802.8	4.3	748	4.1	267
Moneragala	5 545.6	8.6	374	2.1	67
Sabaragamuwa Province	4 948.2	7.7	1 754	9.7	354
Ratnapura	3 255.4	5.1	984	5.4	302
Kegalle	1 692.8	2.6	770	4.3	455
Sri Lanka	64 453.6	100.0	18 112	100.0	281

Source: Department of Census and Statistics.

[a/] Excluding large inland waters.

Table C.1 Numerical distribution of the enumerated population by five-year age group and sex: census years of 1953 to 1981

Age group	1953		1963		1971		1981	
	Male	Female	Male	Female	Male	Female	Male	Female
0-4	609 020	599 809	815 560	783 580	845 463	819 215	944 503	910 235
5-9	550 022	535 892	736 210	724 480	846 831	824 085	855 716	826 811
10-14	474 739	445 447	681 860	650 360	820 950	788 140	862 305	827 028
15-19	364 432	339 412	520 850	501 800	688 715	671 248	812 798	790 389
20-24	395 165	372 307	440 270	444 250	639 574	631 115	765 617	760 846
25-29	371 205	337 666	376 280	371 530	478 970	475 188	638 025	636 832
30-34	285 303	235 482	354 340	316 460	377 745	352 034	569 613	555 813
35-39	292 138	243 452	339 580	309 700	366 884	358 567	421 697	417 376
40-44	210 565	161 475	258 300	211 740	314 343	271 876	359 944	338 259
45-49	211 357	158 959	247 300	197 290	289 638	255 170	308 742	300 547
50-54	159 664	118 490	192 440	153 020	227 034	190 991	284 568	254 956
55-59	108 944	79 681	156 060	114 060	192 183	157 305	222 326	199 996
60-64	83 958	69 490	140 720	103 200	150 600	117 442	183 338	157 066
65+	152 218	131 603	206 230	172 100	292 430	246 162	339 062	302 342
Unknown	–	–	36 850	33 640	–	–	–	–
All ages	4 268 730	3 829 165	5 502 850	5 087 210	6 531 360	6 158 538	7 568 254	7 278 496

Source: Department of Census and Statistics.

Table C.2 Percentage distribution of the enumerated population by five-year age group and sex: census years of 1953 to 1981

Age group	1953		1963		1971		1981	
	Male	Female	Male	Female	Male	Female	Male	Female
0-4	14.3	15.7	14.9	15.5	12.9	13.3	12.5	12.5
5-9	12.9	14.0	13.5	14.3	13.0	13.4	11.3	11.4
10-14	11.1	11.6	12.5	12.9	12.6	12.8	11.4	11.4
15-19	8.5	8.8	9.5	9.9	10.5	10.9	10.7	10.9
20-24	9.2	9.7	8.1	8.8	9.8	10.2	10.1	10.5
25-29	8.8	8.8	6.9	7.4	7.3	7.7	8.4	8.7
30-34	6.7	6.2	6.5	6.3	5.8	5.7	7.5	7.6
35-39	6.8	6.4	6.2	6.1	5.6	5.8	5.6	5.7
40-44	4.9	4.2	4.7	4.2	4.8	4.4	4.8	4.6
45-49	5.0	4.2	4.5	3.9	4.4	4.1	4.1	4.1
50-54	3.7	3.1	3.5	3.0	3.5	3.1	3.8	3.5
55-59	2.6	2.1	2.9	2.3	2.9	2.6	2.9	2.7
60-64	1.9	1.8	2.6	2.0	2.3	1.9	2.4	2.2
65+	3.7	3.4	3.8	3.4	4.5	4.0	4.5	4.2
All ages	100.0	100.0	100.0	100.0	100.0	100.0	100.0	100.0

Source: Department of Census and Statistics.

Table C.3 Numerical distribution of persons aged 15 years and over by marital status and sex: census years of 1946 to 1981

Sex/census year	Never married	Married	Widowed	Divorced/separated	All marital status
Both sexes					
1946	1 308 964	2 494 851	363 011	12 069	4 178 895
1953	1 510 367	2 953 132	398 841	20 626	4 882 966
1963	2 102 248	3 666 194	405 461	18 506	6 192 409
1971	2 922 632	4 353 854	427 649	41 077	7 745 212
1981	3 610 531	5 491 511	467 715	50 395	9 620 152
Male					
1946	903 083	1 264 410	95 341	5 500	2 268 334
1953	1 026 270	1 493 280	105 575	9 824	2 634 949
1963	1 331 208	1 827 209	104 807	8 127	3 271 351
1971	1 755 607	2 152 330	92 769	17 410	4 018 116
1981	2 085 222	2 709 283	90 516	20 709	4 905 730
Female					
1946	405 881	1 230 441	267 670	6 569	1 910 561
1953	484 097	1 459 852	293 266	10 802	2 248 017
1963	771 040	1 838 985	300 654	10 379	2 921 058
1971	1,167 025	2 201 524	334 880	23 667	3 727 096
1981	1 525 309	2 782 228	377 199	29 686	4 714 422

Source: Department of Census and Statistics.

Table C.4 Drop-out rates up to year 9 in government schools by province, district and sex: 1991/92

Province/district	Both sexes	Boys	Girls
Western Province	**2.6**	**2.5**	**2.7**
Colombo	2.3	1.4	3.3
Gampaha	2.4	2.9	1.9
Kalutara	3.3	3.9	2.8
Central Province	**3.7**	**4.2**	**3.2**
Kandy	3.0	3.4	2.5
Matale	4.0	4.5	3.5
Nuwara Eliya	4.7	5.2	4.0
Southern Province	**2.8**	**3.5**	**2.0**
Galle	3.1	3.6	2.7
Matara	2.0	2.8	1.2
Hambantota	3.1	4.0	2.1
Northern Province	**11.0**	**12.2**	**9.7**
Jaffna	9.7	11.0	8.3
Kilinochchi	0.5	1.3	0.3
Mannar	31.8	33.0	30.4
Mullaitivu	16.7	17.4	15.9
Vavuniya	10.9	12.2	9.5
Eastern Province	**4.8**	**4.8**	**4.8**
Batticaloa	7.6	8.2	6.9
Ampara	3.9	3.8	4.1
Trincomalee	2.7	2.1	3.2
North-Western Province	**4.0**	**4.6**	**3.4**
Kurunegala	3.0	3.7	2.3
Puttalam	6.1	6.5	5.7
North-Central Province	**3.9**	**4.5**	**3.3**
Anuradhapura	3.5	4.1	2.9
Polonnaruwa	4.8	5.5	4.1
Uva Province	**3.0**	**3.7**	**2.3**
Badulla	2.8	3.5	2.1
Moneragala	3.4	4.1	2.7
Sabaragamuwa Province	**3.5**	**4.2**	**2.9**
Ratnapura	3.9	4.3	2.9
Kegalle	3.0	3.2	2.8
Sri Lanka	**3.9**	**4.4**	**3.5**

Source: Ministry of Education and Higher Education, cited in Department of Census and Statistics, *Statistical Abstract of the Demogratic Socialist Republic of Sri Lanka, 1995.*

Table C.5 Trainees in vocational training courses under the National Apprenticeship and Industrial Training Authority, by type of course and sex: 1992

Training course	Craft apprenticeship scheme		Village-level apprenticeship	
	Both sexes	Percentage female	Both sexes	Percentage female
Automotive trades	82	–	139	–
Building trades	3	–	31	–
Electrical trades	58	6.9	89	13.5
Electronic and telecommunication trades	69	26.1	44	11.4
Gem and jewellery industry trades	201	56.7	12	33.3
Metal forming and machining trades	67	3.0	54	–
Operative trades	298	2.3	21	42.8
Office machinery and precision equipment trades	4	–	10	40.0
Rubber and plastic products trades	16	50.0	6	50.0
Shoe and leather goods trades	55	78.2	35	82.8
Textile and garment industry trades	663	91.1	704	90.8
Woodworking trades	73	23.3	157	4.4
Clerical and allied trades	239	81.2	21	85.7
Services	345	76.8	571	96.5
Agricultural and industrial trades	149	23.5	57	56.1
Telecommunication trades	2	100.0	–	–
Hotel and catering trades	42	59.5	3	–
Fitting and fabricating trades	91	–	136	–
Painting and finishing trades	22	50.0	4	25.0
Printing trades	177	33.9	49	49.0
All ages	2 656	53.0	2 143	62.4

Source: Tertiary and Vocational Training Commission.

Table C.6 Distribution of university undergraduate students by faculty and sex: selected years, 1966/67 to 1991/92

Faculty	1966/67		1975/76		1985/86		1991/92	
	Male	Female	Male	Female	Male	Female	Male	Female
Medicine	1 105	446	655	584	1 339	1 006	2 207	1 662
Dentistry	59	36	85	108	128	161	195	212
Veterinary science	60	10	55	53	97	73	146	115
Agriculture	72	11	290	100	496	279	841	676
Engineering	560	11	1 084	126	1 498	264	2 705	377
Architecture	25	–	52	21	59	49	111	100
Science	605	197	1 137	660	1 819	1 306	3 274	2 330
Management studies	–	–	626	263	1 941	1 426	3 105	2 450
Law	53	19	83	61	242	219	398	526
Social science and humanities[a]	6 346	4 556	3 429	3 176	3 124	3 377	4 063	5 144
Total	**8 885**	**5 286**	**7 496**	**5 152**	**10 743**	**8 160**	**17 045**	**13 592**
Total professional science[b]	1 881	514	2 221	992	3 617	1 832	6 205	3 142
Total science[c]	605	197	1 137	660	1 819	1 306	3 274	2 330
Total arts-based[d]	6 399	4 575	4 138	3 500	5 307	5 022	7 566	8 120

Sources: Kumari Jayawardena and Swarna Jayaweera, "The integration of women in development planning: Sri Lanka", in Noeleen Heyzer, ed., *Missing Women: Development Planning in Asia and the Pacific* (Kuala Lumpur, Asian and Pacific Development Centre, 1985); and Swarna Jayaweera, "Women and education" in Centre for Women's Research, *Facets of Change: Women in Sri Lanka, 1985-1995* (Colombo, July 1995).

[a] Including education.

[b] Comprising medicine, dentistry, veterinary science, agriculture, engineering and architecture.

[c] Comprising science.

[d] Comprising management studies, law, social sciences and humanities.

92

Table C.7 Infant mortality rates by district and sex: 1970, 1980 and 1988

Province/district	1970			1980			1988		
	Both sexes	Male	Female	Both sexes	Male	Female	Both sexes	Male	Female
Western Province									
Colombo	41.7	45.9	37.3	47.7	53.6	41.6	24.6	27.4	21.7
Gampaha	–	–	–	24.0	26.3	21.7	14.9	16.3	13.4
Kalutara	44.3	45.8	42.7	30.3	31.7	28.9	15.4	15.8	14.9
Central Province									
Kandy	57.0	60.9	53.0	54.7	58.9	50.3	29.1	32.1	25.8
Matale	47.6	51.5	43.5	24.8	26.9	22.5	14.9	16.7	13.0
Nuwara Eliya	94.5	104.4	83.7	73.8	80.5	66.8	35.5	38.6	32.3
Southern Province									
Galle	48.7	54.7	42.5	39.2	42.0	36.3	18.5	19.0	18.1
Matara	41.6	47.4	35.7	33.8	36.1	31.5	21.7	21.3	22.1
Hambantota	36.4	39.5	33.1	22.4	23.3	21.6	8.2	8.2	8.1
Northern Province									
Jaffna	30.8	33.1	28.5	18.0	20.3	15.7	21.1	23.6	18.4
Kilinochchi	–	–	–	–	–	–	11.4	8.3	14.8
Mannar	49.1	50.5	47.5	25.4	29.5	21.3	16.9	16.7	17.2
Mullaitivu	–	–	–	17.0	20.5	13.4	23.3	22.2	24.4
Vavuniya	42.5	44.6	41.0	16.3	21.2	11.3	15.6	14.0	17.4
Eastern Province									
Batticaloa	57.7	60.7	54.6	34.1	37.3	30.5	8.5	8.3	8.7
Ampara	44.8	48.2	41.2	20.3	21.5	19.0	12.6	12.8	12.5
Trincomalee	36.9	37.7	36.0	19.1	18.8	19.5	9.3	8.0	10.6
North-Western Province									
Kurunegala	42.8	48.3	37.2	29.9	33.3	26.4	21.6	24.8	18.1
Puttalam	48.4	54.4	42.6	20.8	22.6	18.9	14.3	15.0	13.5
North-Central Province									
Anuradhapura	38.8	39.1	38.6	16.7	18.3	15.1	24.9	26.2	23.5
Polonnaruwa	33.2	34.4	32.0	18.6	21.9	14.9	11.3	11.1	11.6
Uva Province									
Badulla	60.6	65.7	55.3	46.6	50.0	43.4	24.2	25.9	22.4
Moneragala	39.6	41.4	37.7	15.6	15.7	15.5	7.0	6.9	7.1
Sabaragamuwa Province									
Ratnapura	64.3	69.6	58.7	43.3	46.4	40.1	26.0	27.9	23.9
Kegalle	49.6	53.7	43.4	30.7	33.0	28.3	12.4	14.6	10.1
Sri Lanka	47.5	51.5	43.3	34.4	37.4	31.3	20.2	21.7	18.5

Source: Registrar General's Department.

93

Table D.1 Percentage of currently married women by current use of contraception and background characteristics: 1993

Background characteristic	Current use of contraception				
	Not currently using	Using modern temporary	Sterilized	Using traditional methods	Total
Sector					
Colombo metro	37.3	16.2	21.5	25.1	100.0
Other urban	42.3	16.0	20.8	20.8	100.0
Rural	31.7	17.6	27.6	23.2	100.0
Estate	45.5	3.1	44.4	7.0	100.0
Zone					
Zone 1	37.3	16.2	21.5	25.1	100.0
Zone 2	28.9	17.4	23.7	29.9	100.0
Zone 3	36.0	16.0	20.6	27.4	100.0
Zone 4	32.4	16.2	26.6	24.6	100.0
Zone 5	36.3	15.7	36.9	11.2	100.0
Zone 6	32.8	19.5	36.1	15.9	100.0
Zone 7	34.1	16.2	28.6	21.2	100.0
Education					
No education	41.8	7.2	40.6	10.4	100.0
Primary	31.1	11.8	41.4	15.7	100.0
Secondary	32.2	18.2	26.4	23.2	100.0
More than secondary	36.0	20.3	14.4	29.2	100.0
Total	33.9	16.5	27.2	22.4	100.0

Source: Department of Census and Statistics, *Sri Lanka Demographic and Health Survey, 1993* (Colombo, February 1995).

Table E.1 Total population and economically active population aged 10 years and over by activity status and sex: 1963-1996

Census/survey year and gender	Total population 10 years and over	Labour force or economically active persons 10 years and over			Persons 10+ not in the labour force
		Employed	Unemployed	Total	
1963					
Both sexes	7 453 899	3 158 452	263 869	3 422 321	4 031 578
Male	3 916 366	2 514 088	199 691	2 713 779	1 202 587
Female	3 537 623	644 364	64 178	708 542	2 829 081.
1971					
Both sexes	9 354 303	3 648 875	839 264	4 488 139	4 866 164
Male	4 839 067	2 838 404	474 065	3 312 469	1 526 598
Female	4 515 236	810 471	365 199	1 175 670	3 339 566
1981					
Both sexes	11 309 485	4 119 324	895 143	5 014 467	6 295 018
Male	5 768 035	3 248 448	498 726	3 747 174	2 020 861
Female	5 541 450	870 876	396 417	1 267 293	4 274 157
1985/86					
Both sexes	11 868 919	5 131 749	840 252	5 972 001	5 896 918
Male	5 851 930	3 581 341	433 243	4 014 584	1 837 346
Female	6 016 989	1 550 407	407 009	1 957 416	4 059 573
1992[a/]					
Both sexes	12 059 472	4 924 275	832 397	5 756 672	6 302 800
Male	6 029 908	3 464 559	415 043	3 879 602	2 150 306
Female	6 029 564	1 459 716	417 354	1 877 070	4 152 494
1995 (First Quarter)[a/]					
Both sexes	12 719 720	5 315 967	759 099	6 075 066	6 644 654
Male	6 289 656	3 660 993	352 891	4 013 884	2 275 772
Female	6 430 064	1 654 974	406 208	2 061 182	4 368 882
1996 (First Quarter)[a/]					
Both sexes	12 810 100	5 586 917	710 251	6 297 168	6 512 932
Male	6 317 982	3 797 422	328 223	4 125 645	2 192 337
Female	6 492 118	1 789 495	382 028	2 171 523	4 320 595

Sources: Department of Census and Statistics, reports of the censuses of population and housing, 1963, 1971 and 1981; and reports of the Sri Lanka Labour Force Survey, 1985/86, 1992, 1995 and 1996.

[a/] Relating to household population only. The 1992, 1995 and 1996 Surveys do not cover the Northern and Eastern provinces.

REFERENCES

Abeykoon, A.T.P.L. (1995), "Sex preference in South Asia: Sri Lanka an outlier", *Asia-Pacific Population Journal*, vol. 10, No. 3.

Canagaretnam, I.T. (1992), "Role of the enforcement authorities in the prevention of violence against women", paper presented at the Workshop on Violence Against Women (Colombo, Women's Bureau).

Centre for Women's Research (1995), *Facets of Change: Women in Sri Lanka, 1986-1995* (Colombo, July).

Department of Census and Statistics (1995), Ministry of Finance and Planning, *Sri Lanka Demographic and Health Survey, 1993* (Colombo, February).

――――, *Sri Lanka Labour Force Survey, 1992; Final Report* (Colombo, February).

――――, *Women and Men in Sri Lanka* (Colombo, May).

――――, *Quarterly Report of the Sri Lanka Labour Force Survey: First Quarter, 1995* (Colombo, August).

――――, *Statistical Abstract of the Democratic Socialist Republic of Sri Lanka, 1995* (Colombo, October).

――――(1996), *National Household Survey, 1993, Sri Lanka: Indicators on Selected World Summit Goals for Children and Women: Final Report* (Colombo).

――――(1997), *Changing Role of Women in Sri Lanka* (Colombo, January).

De Silva, W. Indralal (1997), "Ireland of Asia: trends in marriage timing in Sri Lanka", *Asia-Pacific Population Journal*, vol. 12, No. 2, June.

De Silva, Wimala (1995), "Political participation of women in Sri Lanka, 1985-1995", in Centre for Women's Research, *Facets of Change: Women in Sri Lanka, 1986-1995 (Colombo, July).*

Dias Malsiri and Nedra Weerakoon (1995), "Migrant women domestic workers from Sri Lanka – trends and issues", in Centre for Women's Research, *Facets of Change: Women in Sri Lanka, 1986-1995* (Colombo, July).

Dissanayake, Lakshman (1997), "Factors influencing stabilization of women's age at marriage in Sri Lanka" (draft), (University of Adelaide, Australia).

Economist Intelligence Unit (1996), *Country Profile: Sri Lanka, 1995-1996* (London).

Economic and Social Commission for Asia and the Pacific (1976), *Population of Sri Lanka*, Country Monograph Series No. 4 (ST/ESCAP/30) (Bangkok).

――――(1994), *Human Resources Development: Effectiveness of Programme Delivery at the Local Level in Countries of the ESCAP Region*, Development Papers No. 16 (ST/ESCAP/1296) (Bangkok).

――――(1996), *Socio-economic Profile of SAARC Countries: A Statistical Analysis*, Statistical Profiles No. 1 (ST/ESCAP/1537) (Bangkok).

Fernando, Dallas F.S. (1975), "Changing nuptiality patterns in Sri Lanka, 1901-1971". *Population Studies* (London), vol. 29, No. 2.

Gunasekara, H.R. (1996), *Nutritional Status of Children in Sri Lanka*, Demographic and Health Survey, Further Analysis Series No. 1 (Colombo, Department of Census and Statistics, July).

Jayawardena, Kumari and Swarna Jayaweera (1985), "The integration of women in development planning: Sri Lanka" in Noeleen Heyzer, ed., *Missing Women:*

Development Planning in Asia and the Pacific (Kuala Lumpur, Asian and Pacific Development Centre).

Jayawardene, C.H.S. and S. Selvaratnam, "Fertility levels and trends in Ceylon", paper presented at the International Union for the Scientific Study of Population Conference, Sydney, August 1967.

Jayaweera, Swarna (1995), "Women and education", in Centre for Women's Research, *Facets of Change: Women in Sri Lanka, 1986-1995,* (Colombo, July).

Ministry of Transport, Environment and Women's Affairs, *National Plan of Action for Women in Sri Lanka: Towards Gender Equality* (undated).

Nadarajah, T. (1983), "The transition from higher female to higher male mortality to Sri Lanka". *Population and Development Review,* vol. 9, No. 2, June.

Selvaratnam S. (1988), "Population and status of Women", *Asia-Pacific Population Journal,* vol. 3, No. 2.

———— (1990), "Mortality experience in Sri Lanka", in K. Mahadevan, ed., *Policies and Strategies for Child Survival: Experiences from Asia* (Delhi, B.R. Publishing Corporation).

United Nations (1995), *Living Arrangements of Women and Their Children in Developing Countries: A Demographic Profile* (New York, Department for Economic and Social Information and Policy Analysis) (ST/ESA/SER.R/141).

———— (1996), *World Population Prospects: The 1996 Revision, Annexes II and III: Demographic Indicators by Major Areas, Region and Country* (Department of Economic and Social Information and Policy Analysis, October) (forthcoming).

United Nations Educational, Scientific and Cultural Organization (1984), *Towards Universalization of Primary Education in Asia and* the Pacific, *Country Studies: Sri Lanka* (Bangkok, UNESCO Regional Office for Education in Asia and the Pacific).

United Nations Children's Fund (1991), *Children and Women in Sri Lanka: A Situation Analysis* (Colombo).

Wijayatilake, Kamlini (1995), "Violence against women – Review of a decade", in Centre for Women's Research, *Facets of Change: Women in Sri Lanka, 1986-1995* (Colombo, July).

Wilson, Pitiyage (1975), *Economic Implications of Population Growth: Sri Lanka Labour Force (1946-1981)* (Canberra, The Australian National University).

Women's Affairs Division, Sri Lanka (1994), *Towards Gender Equity: The Sri Lanka National Report to the 1995 United Nations Fourth World Conference on Women* (Colombo, Ministry of Transport, Environment and Women's Affairs, November).

World Bank (1995), *Sri Lanka Poverty Assessment,* Report, No. 13431-CE (Washington D.C).